The Final Frontier

Possessing the Land

Richard Crisco

Revival Press

An Imprint of
Destiny Image® Publishers, Inc.
P.O. Box 310
Shippensburg, PA 17257-0310

ISBN 0-7684-2003-2

For Worldwide Distribution
Printed in the U.S.A.

Cover by Epoch Designs

This book and all other Destiny Image, Revival Press,
and Treasure House books are available
at Christian bookstores and distributors worldwide.

For a U.S. bookstore nearest you, call **1-800-722-6774**.
For more information on foreign distributors, call **717-532-3040**.
Or reach us on the Internet: **http://www.reapernet.com**

Dedication

To Jane, my godly wife, for always being there to pray for me and believe in me, even when I have a hard time believing in myself.

To Ashley and Caleb, my wonderful children, for the joy and inspiration they bring to my life and home.

To my staff and youth leaders who support me day and night with their unceasing prayers and labors of love. They have pushed me to exercise and develop my own leadership potential.

To Rhonda Nall, my wonderful assistant, who labors endless hours without fanfare or recognition. Thanks for the numerous "extra miles" you have worked to see that everything was done well for the glory of God.

To Jesus, my Master, Savior, and Best Friend.

Acknowledgments

As we journey through life the Lord brings many individuals across our path who make a difference in the way we think and live. I often repeat the prayer of Paul concerning the Philippians: "I thank my God upon every remembrance of you, always in every prayer of mine for you all making request with joy, for your fellowship in the gospel from the first day until now; being confident of this very thing, that He which hath begun a good work in you will perform it until the day of Jesus Christ" (Phil. 1:3-6 KJV).

I am so grateful for my first Senior Pastor, Fred Rogers, who taught me how to love people unconditionally with a shepherd's love. I also greatly appreciate my present Pastor, John Kilpatrick, who birthed in me strong leadership and instructed me in protecting the people from the attacks of the enemy, as well as Evangelist Steve Hill, who resurrected from my weary heart a passion for lost souls and a fresh love to preach the Word with simplicity and power.

I would also like to acknowledge a newer friend who has helped me tremendously through the recent transitions of my life: Jeanne Mayo. Jeanne reminds me of the important and significant things in life. Her godly example provokes me to want to love God and love teenagers more! Thanks, Sis, for "being Jesus with skin on"!

And finally, I thank the radical youth at Brownsville Assembly of God, who help me preach every Thursday night. Their lives, prayers, and love are the coal that feeds my burning passion for this generation. I love you! You are my heroes!

Endorsements

God, give us a new generation who will not only read *The Final Frontier* but also choose to live it! Thanks, Richard, for reminding us that we must have revival in our hearts before we will see it in our world.

Scott Wilson, Founder
New Generation Leadership

Birthed amidst the fire of genuine revival, these messages speak to issues of relevant holiness, aggressive pursuit, and costly commitment. They will challenge you to go beyond the causal and to be a person whose life always speaks louder than your "shout." You'll also soon realize why the Lord chose to place Richard Crisco in Brownsville as the youth pastor. Like few men I know, he has chosen to consistently make his character a much greater issue than his charisma. Indeed, he has conquered his own personal "final frontier."

Jeanne Mayo
Cross Current Youth & Young Adult Director

The Final Frontier is by far the greatest book I have seen on supernatural empowering for youth today. Richard gives practical, day-to-day insight on ways youth can experience the power of the Holy Spirit working in and through their lives. While reading this book I could not help but notice Richard's underlying message that youth are no match for the devil, but that through the power of God working in their lives the devil is no match for them! As a youth leader, I challenge every one of you to read this book, as well as to encourage your teens to read it. The only hope the next generation has is to understand and claim the principles in *The Final Frontier*!

Barry St. Clair
Reach Out Ministries

In each generation God always promises His presence, His power, and His provision. He also promises a priesthood whose responsibility is to hear His voice and then speak prophetically to His people. Richard Crisco is that kind of person. *The Final Frontier* is a trumpet blast to awaken this generation of young people to the power of God and the divine destiny that is in their hands. Every youth pastor or leader in America should read this book from the perspective of the outpouring of the Brownsville Revival. Richard has been in the fire and has a pulse on what God is saying to this generation. God has brought him to the Kingdom for such a time as this.

Johnny Jernigan
Johnny Jernigan Ministries

Youth pastors, get this book, devour every page, and then get a copy into the hands of every spiritually hungry young person you know! Richard Crisco, the leader of the most dedicated, sold out, and on fire youth group I have ever seen, has a message we need to hear. Prepare to be challenged. Prepare to be changed!

Dr. Michael L. Brown
President, Brownsville Revival School of Ministry

Contents

Foreword

I have the privilege of laboring with some of the finest workers in God's harvest field. These choice men and women of God are not only dedicated to the task but also completely committed to every command from the Lord of the harvest. They've counted the cost, and they don't complain when the workload becomes overwhelming. Ian Macpherson once said, "Let me say outright that no man who is not prepared to work himself to death has any right in the ministry at all." I believe his statement hits the bull's eye, and Richard Crisco fits the bill.

Richard Crisco is in love with Jesus and sold out to fulfilling his role in the Great Commission. He is driven by a personal hunger for God that far exceeds every other desire in life. Heaven is continually bombarded with his prayers for the salvation of young people. This young man believes that the youth of today are hungry for the Word of God and are begging for godly leaders who will challenge them to rise up and take a bold stand for Christ. These beliefs have been validated as hundreds flock to his youth services, eager to hear from a man who cares for their souls.

This book serves as an extension of Richard Crisco's ministry. The sermons it contains have been used of God to change, challenge, and charge thousands of young people to live uncompromising, Jesus-filled lives. May they be used of God to pierce your soul and prepare you for the battle ahead.

Stephen Hill
Evangelist

C h a p t e r   1

The Final Frontier
(Part 1)

When you hear the title phrase, "the final frontier," what do you think of? If you are like me and enjoy old Western movies, your imagination may instantly picture scenes with cowboys and Indians, or pioneer families pushing westward in their covered wagons through adverse conditions. If you are a science fiction buff, your mind immediately flashes to scenes similar to those in *Star Wars* or *Star Trek*, where adventures lead beyond the perimeters of our Earth into galaxies of the unknown.

However, this message entitled "The Final Frontier" has nothing to do with the wild West or the adventures of the universe, but rather a small member of our body known as the tongue. I refer to it as the final frontier because the Bible says it is the only thing that man has been unable to conquer or tame (see Jas. 3:8). We've civilized the wild West, captured and tamed every known animal, and conquered the moon and Mars, yet we cannot control our own tongues.

Let's look at what James says about the "final frontier," beginning at chapter 3 and starting with the second part of verse 2:

> *...If anyone is **never at fault in what he says, he is a perfect man,** able to keep his whole body in check.*

> *When we put bits into the mouths of horses to make them obey us, we can turn the whole animal.*

> *Or take ships as an example. Although they are so large and are driven by strong winds, they are steered by a very small rudder wherever the pilot wants to go.*

> *Likewise **the tongue is a small part of the body,** but it makes great boasts. Consider what a great forest is set on fire by a small spark.*

> *The tongue also is a fire, a world of evil among the parts of the body. **It corrupts the whole person,** sets the whole course of his life on fire, and is itself set on fire by hell.*

> *All kinds of animals, birds, reptiles, and creatures of the sea are being tamed and have been tamed by man,*

> ***but no man can tame the tongue....***

There it is, the title of my message, "The Final Frontier." No man can tame—(drum role, please!)—the tongue. Please continue reading from verse 8:

> *...It is a restless evil, full of deadly poison.*

With the tongue we praise our Lord and Father, and with it we curse men, who have been made in God's likeness.

Out of the same mouth come praise and cursing. **My brothers, this should not be.**

Can both fresh water and salt water flow from the same spring?

My brothers, can a fig tree bear olives, or a grapevine bear figs? Neither can a salt spring produce fresh water.

The problem of trying to conquer and control our tongue begins in childhood. Do you remember some of the things you would say when you were little? Things like, *"Tattle-tale, tattle-tale, hang your britches on a nail, hang them high, hang them low, hang them on a buffalo."* Or, *"You missed me, you missed me; now you gotta kiss me."* Or, *"Liar, liar, pants on fire...."* That one ends in several different ways, depending on where you are from.

Here's one we used to say a lot: *"Fatty, fatty, two by four, couldn't get in the bathroom door."* I remember those cute songs that we would sing; those really stupid songs like, *"Johnny and Susie sitting in a tree, k-i-s-s-i-n-g. First comes love, then comes marriage, then comes Johnny with a baby carriage."* Then there were those ridiculous rhymes like, *"Step on a crack and break your mother's back."*

One saying I want us to actually consider is this one: *"Sticks and stones may break my bones, but words will never hurt me."* That is a lie! Words do have the ability to destroy you. Some of you have wounded hearts from words that have been spoken to you. I'm here to tell you that God wants to heal those wounds and set you free.

The tongue is an interesting and powerful part of the body. The Bible says it is the only thing that man can't tame; we can't conquer this little muscle inside of our own mouth. Let me tell you something. Space is *not* the final frontier. It is the boneless tongue—so small and weak, yet able to crush and kill. This, my friends, is what we must conquer. This is the final frontier.

I love one-liners. The ones we've looked at so far in this message have been foolish; but now here are some good ones for you to consider:

"It is better to remain silent and be thought a fool, than to open one's mouth and remove all doubt."

"God gave you two ears and one mouth; thus you should listen twice as much as you speak."

"If your mind goes blank, don't forget to turn off the sound."

"Saving face is often accomplished by keeping the lower part of it shut."

"There is nothing wrong with having nothing to say unless you insist on saying it."

"If no one ever spoke unless he knew what he was talking about, a ghastly hush would descend upon the earth."

"Empty barrels make the loudest noises, but the full ones silently crush one's toes."

I could go on and on with these types of sayings. What they all come down to is the fact that we need to say less more often. The wiser you get, probably the less you talk. Here is what Proverbs 17:27-28 tells us:

A man of knowledge uses words with restraint, and a man of understanding is even-tempered.

Even a fool is thought wise if he keeps silent, and discerning if he holds his tongue.

What is the writer saying here? He is saying that the wiser you get, the fewer words you are going to use.

I want you to understand something important about your tongue: It reveals who you are.

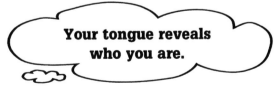

Your tongue reveals who you are.

Let's take a look at Matthew 12:33-37.

Make a tree good and its fruit will be good, or make a tree bad and its fruit will be bad, for a tree is recognized by its fruit.

*You brood of vipers, how can you who are evil say anything good? For **out of the overflow of the heart the mouth speaks.***

The good man brings good things out of the good stored up in him, and the evil man brings evil things out of the evil stored up in him.

*But I tell you that men will have to **give account on the day of judgment for every careless word** they have spoken.*

*For **by your words you will be acquitted, and by your words you will be condemned.***

Notice in these verses how it says that out of the overflow, or out of the abundance, of the heart the mouth speaks. Listen, if you have a hard time with gossiping, then it tells me that there is a lot of wickedness in your heart. If you have a hard time with cutting people down, with back-stabbing people and cussing, then what you are telling me is that there is a lot of crud in your heart. Words come out of the overflow and abundance of what is really inside your heart.

People can become experts at trying to hide what is going on inside them. They can build good reputations and have others speak highly of them. Young person, let me tell you the way to know what someone is really like: Sit around that person for a while and just listen to what he or she says about other people. Listen to how that person talks and consider the content of his conversation. You will learn more about who someone is by what he is saying about others than by what other people say about him. Our tongues reveal who we are.

You can tell more about a person by what he says about others than by what others say about him.

What a person says to me reveals his or her character. Let me explain that statement. Don't come up to me and say, "Brother Richard, people are all the time inviting me out to parties. They are all the time tempting me to go to bed. They are all the time wanting me to get drunk. They are all the time wanting me to go get high. They are all the time asking me to do things that are wrong." Do you know what you are telling me? You are telling me that you are not the strong Christian you would like me to think you are. You are telling me that you are not living the life you should at school and around your friends.

Listen, when God got hold of me just before I went into my senior year, my life was totally changed. Earlier in high school, I had been one of the party animals. But let me tell you, after I gave my life to Jesus, I never had another person invite me out to go get high. I never had another person invite me out to go get drunk or to get involved in parties or anything else. Do you know why? It was because my character had changed, and the people around me could see it.

Some of you cry and scream and bellyache about peer pressure. If you will start living the life, it will deal with that peer pressure. Let people know where you stand. If somebody comes and starts telling you a dirty joke, just point to your head and say, "What's this look like? A garbage can? Stop putting your trash in my ears!" If you do that one or two times, people will get the message.

If you ever complain to me about how people all the time come and tell you the latest gossip, how they come and tell you the latest trash in the youth group, how they come and tempt you, do you know what you are doing? You are telling me that you have poor character. People don't tell me trash, and it is not because I'm the youth pastor. Many of my young people will tell you that they don't hear trash either. Do you know why? It is because they live godly lives and people know that a godly person doesn't want to hear other people's trash.

The tongue is the most powerful weapon given to man. It can be used to build or destroy. It can be used to bless or curse. It can be used to kill or bring life. Proverbs 18:21 says:

*The **tongue has the power of life and death,** and those who love it will eat its fruit.*

> **Some people should have their tongues registered with the local police department as lethal weapons.**

The power of life and death… Some people should have their tongues registered with the local police department as lethal weapons. Some of you young people have very sharp and destructive tongues. And girls, I pick on the guys a lot, but I'm sorry to tell you that in this department you probably win the award. Girls, you've got tongues that can rip a guy to pieces and you don't even realize it.

Contrary to popular belief, I'm still a young man. I'm only 36, but when I start talking about stuff that happened 20 years ago, it makes me sound ancient. Anyway, I vividly remember 20 years ago sitting in a typing class in front of a group of about six girls who were going at it. I think they were probably laughing behind my back, and they were talking just loud enough for me to hear. In tenth grade I had yet to kiss my first girl. Jesus spared me. You have to understand that, for me, kissing was a major traumatic thing. I remember even having a dream about kissing a girl. I was so excited because I finally had done it. When I woke up, it was horrendous. I was so depressed. Now here I am sitting in class. I am already petrified by these things called girls. And these girls are sitting behind me ripping guys to pieces. They are saying things like, "So-and-so is sloppy." "So-and-so is dry." They were talking about the way different guys kissed and their conversation was like fuel to my paranoia. They were killing me inside.

Again, Proverbs 18:21: "The tongue has the power of life and death...." The power of life and death? How can our tongues kill? As I have studied and meditated on this, I've learned that one of the ways in which our tongues can bring death is through gossip.

The definition of gossip is "idle talk or chatter." Earlier we read Matthew 12:36 where it says that one day we will answer for every careless, idle word we have spoken. You need to recognize that your words are eternal. When you stand before Jesus Christ on judgment day, you will give account for every careless word that you ever spoke. That's not Richard speaking; that's the Word of God speaking.

Proverbs 18:8 tells us,

*The words of a gossip are like choice morsels; they go **down to a man's inmost parts.***

I want you to understand something. When you gossip, when you slander someone, when you talk about someone, the Scriptures say those words go to the innermost parts of that person. Have you ever had somebody say things about you and you could feel the pain of those words going deep inside you? Sharp words cut right to the heart. That's what the Scriptures say.

Proverbs 20:19 states that,

*A gossip betrays a confidence; so **avoid a man who talks too much.***

One time a lady, the biggest gossiper in her church, heard an especially juicy tidbit about her pastor. After she had passed the story on to a number of people in town, she found out that the rumor was false. The lady went to her pastor to apologize and ask for his forgiveness. She said that she would go back to all the people and tell them it was just a false story.

The pastor agreed to forgive her, but he said that he wanted her to do something for him. He told her to go and get a sack full of chicken feathers, take it to the main intersection of town, throw those feathers into the wind, and then come back and report to him. The lady thought it was a strange request and hesitated, but agreed to do it anyway. She did as her pastor requested and then went back to his office. "Now," said the pastor, "go back downtown and gather all those feathers again."

The lady replied, "But pastor, there is no way I could ever do that. The wind has carried them all over town." The pastor smiled sadly and said, "That's true. It's the same way when you tell a story about someone else. There is no way to go around and take back what has been said."

When you begin to spread a rumor, when you begin to speak something negative about someone, there is no way to take it back. Have you ever noticed how bad news always travels faster than good news? Have you ever noticed how slander seems to just flow through some communities and even some churches? Why is that? The reason is that we are deceitfully wicked.

We love juicy trash about somebody else because it makes us feel good. It puffs us up whenever we slander somebody else. It makes us feel like we are better than him. Let me tell you who usually gets it: the popular one. It is usually the leader. It is usually the person who is well-liked. If that person makes the slightest mistake, everybody jumps on him. Why does that happen? It is because pulling that person down through slander makes everyone else feel good and comfortable about themselves.

Why do people attack authority figures? Why do teenagers and rebellious adults slander police officers? Why do they call them pigs and hogs? Why do they do that? I'll tell you why. Tearing down authority makes them feel like they are something big and macho. They don't tear at somebody who is equal to them; they always pick someone higher. To me, this fact is one of the greatest proofs that Jesus Christ is Lord, that He is the one and only Lord and authority over Heaven and earth.

Have you ever noticed that when people cuss, they always use the Lord's name in vain? I've never yet heard anybody say, "Oh, for Buddha's sake, shut up." Think about it. "For Mohammed's sake, shut up." "For Hare Krishna's sake, leave me alone." It sounds stupid, doesn't it? Do you know why? It is because there is no authority in those names. It is always the name of Jesus Christ that is used.

So the next time you need some proof for a skeptic or two, you have it. Ask them why people don't cuss in any other god's name. Ask them why it is always Jesus' name. Why? It's because Jesus is the ultimate authority and mankind thinks that they are big shots—just because with their stinking tongues and with the very breath that He gave them, they can slander Jesus' name. The hammer is going to come down on that tongue one day.

Let's go back to the gossip issue. Maybe you have friends who are all the time coming to you and talking about other people. Trust me. If they come to you and talk about somebody, when they get through doing that, they are going right back to somebody else and talking about you. You need to cut ties with those kind of friends. They will get you in trouble.

All gossips ought to be hung—one by the ear, the other by the tongue.

I love this saying, which I picked up several years ago: "All gossips ought to be hung—one by the ear, the other by the tongue." It takes two people to gossip. And don't come to me with some juicy tidbit about someone and say, "Brother Richard, it's true." *So what?* "But Brother Richard, if it is true, then don't I have the right to repeat it?" I want to ask you a question: "W-W-J-D?" Most of you know what those letters stand for. *What would Jesus do?* Think about what He did in the Scriptures.

In John chapter 8, after the woman got caught in adultery, did Jesus go around talking about how this naked woman was dragged before His feet and... No. Jesus never talked about her again. Did Jesus, after Peter denied Him three times (see Lk. 22), go around and constantly bring it up? "You can't depend on Peter; he will deny you." No. Did He go around when Thomas doubted the resurrection (see Jn. 20) and slander Thomas? No. Let me ask you this: When you blow it in sin, does Jesus go around talking about you? No. He chooses to forgive and forget. The fact that something might be true does not give you the license to go around and continually dig up the trash and spew it all over the church or the community.

Let's look at Philippians 4:8 in the King James Version:

*Finally, brethren, whatsoever things are true, whatsoever things are honest, whatsoever things are just, whatsoever things are pure, whatsoever things are lovely, whatsoever things are of good report; **if** there be any virtue, and **if** there be any praise, think on these things.*

If. Now the word *if* is only two letters long, but it is the biggest word in that verse. *If* there be any virtue and *if* there be any praise, think on these things. Only repeat what will bring virtue, praise, and glory to the Lord Jesus Christ and what will build up His people.

There are a few questions I want you to ask yourself before you open your mouth to talk about someone:

1. "What is my motive for saying this thing? Why do I want to say it?" Too many times we say things because, again, we are trying to make ourselves look good or feel important; or because we want to get even with somebody. What is your motive for saying what you are about to say?

2. "Would Jesus say this?" That's the best question right there. Would Jesus repeat this story? Would Jesus rehearse this event?

3. "What good will result from my saying this? Is there anything good that could come out of this conversation?" If not, keep your mouth shut, because the devil will use everything he can to destroy.

4. "Would I want somebody else to say this about me?" Now we are hitting home. Is what you are about to say something that you would want somebody else to say about you? If the tables were reversed and you were the one on the gossip end, would this be something you would want everybody else talking about?

5. "Will this bring life or death?" What will be the result of your opening your mouth? Will it bring life or death to another person's inner self?

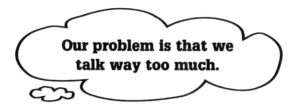

Our problem is that we
talk way too much.

We talk way too much. Let's look at some more Scriptures. Proverbs 10:19—what an incredible verse:

When words are many, sin is not absent, *but he who holds his tongue is wise.*

You will notice that many of the Scriptures I use in my messages come out of the Book of Proverbs. I recommend that young people read through it every month, because it is loaded with incredible character verses. Look at 10:19 one more time.

When words are many, sin is not absent....

We get into trouble when we talk too much. Proverbs 26:20 says this:

Without wood a fire goes out....

I know that is real deep. It might be hard for some of you to understand. Let's read it again:

Without wood a fire goes out; without gossip a quarrel dies down.

Isn't that good? Isn't that revolutionary? Without wood a fire goes out. Without gossip a quarrel dies.

I want to bring out one last observation before I leave the gossip issue. Many of the people who think everybody is talking about them believe it is true, not because people are actually talking about them, but because they are talking about other people.

> **You don't see things as they really are; you see things as you are.**

I've had young people through the years who constantly complain, "Somebody is talking about me." I learned that what is really happening is this: If Susie and Johnny have a problem, and Susie and Janie have a problem, and Susie and Bill have a problem, then Susie is the problem. Are you with me? You and I think that we see things clearly, but we don't. We see things through the eyes of our own understanding and not as they really are. We see things as *we* are.

There are some people who think that everybody is talking about them. First of all, although I hate to burst your bubble, you are not that important. Everybody doesn't wake up in the morning and go, "I wonder how Susie is doing today?" "I wonder how Johnny is doing today?" I'm sorry. I know that you think you are high and mighty and that the world revolves around you and that your youth group would fall apart without you, but you are just not that important. You might think that you are, but you are not. People don't go around all day long wanting to talk about you. We are all too busy for that.

Secondly, here's what I learned. You think that everybody is talking about you because you think that everybody is like you. And because you talk about everybody else, you assume that everybody else is talking about you. You think that everybody is mean to you. The truth of the matter is that you are the one who is mean. You say, "Everybody is a hypocrite; everybody in the whole church is a hypocrite." The truth of the matter is that *you* are the hypocrite. I heard a phrase one time that says, *"It takes one to know one."*

The way that you see other people reveals who you are. So if you are one of those people who thinks that everybody is always talking about you, then, my friend, you have just revealed something about yourself.

As Christians, we often talk big about winning our school or city for Jesus. We love to dance and shout about the great things we are going to accomplish for the Kingdom of God. We gloat with pride as we sing about how the devil is under our feet. But the greatest victory of all is when we learn to die to ourselves and allow Jesus to be in full control of our lives, including what comes out of our mouths.

There is a lot of truth in the old saying, *"I have met the enemy, and the enemy is me."* Perhaps, as we have been exploring this final frontier, it has been revealed to you that there are areas of wickedness in your life. Maybe you thought that you were doing well until now, but as you have paused to listen to words that have been spoken by your own tongue, it has revealed poisons stored within the chambers of your heart. If that is true, then I want you to join with me in a prayer of repentance and surrender:

Dear Jesus, I confess today that I have a wicked tongue and that its roots are deep within my sinful heart. I ask that You forgive me of my sin. Cleanse my heart. Take control of my life, my heart, my tongue. May my thoughts be Your thoughts and my words Your words. Fill my mouth with words of life, love, hope, and faith. May I glorify You in everything I say and do. In Jesus' name, amen.

The Final Frontier
(Part 2)

The tongue has the power of life and death....
Proverbs 18:21

Let's do some more exploration in this "final frontier." Our tongues will speak life into every circumstance when they fulfill the purposes for which they were created. Why were our tongues created? What makes them so important? What is their real purpose?

1. The purpose of our tongues is for praise and worship.

First Peter chapter 2 verse 9 (KJV) says,

But ye are a chosen generation, a royal priesthood, an holy nation, a peculiar people; that ye should show forth the praises of Him who hath called you out of darkness into His marvellous light.

Although I am not going to expand on this area in this particular message, the tongue's highest calling is to speak and sing the praises of God. When we worship the Lord, we are set free; we are liberated. Life is poured into us as a result of praise and worship.

2. The purpose of our tongues is to witness.

Acts 1:8 (KJV) says,

But ye shall receive power, after that the Holy Ghost is come upon you: and ye shall be witnesses unto Me both in Jerusalem, and in all Judaea, and in Samaria, and unto the uttermost part of the earth.

Your tongue was created so that you might witness and tell of the wondrous things that God has done for you. I love to preach on evangelism, but I'm not going to right now. I want us to move into other areas where we're going to do some serious exploring. The things I'm about to share with you are very valuable in the practical, everyday conquest of our "final frontier."

3. The purpose of our tongues is to encourage and edify; to build up and strengthen other people.

I remember, right before revival hit Brownsville in the summer of 1995, that I was doing a series on the subject of "time." That is when I noticed Colossians chapter 4, a very interesting portion of Scripture. Colossians 4 verse 5 in both the King James Version and the New International Version says,

*Walk in wisdom toward them that are without, **redeeming the time**.*

*Be wise in the way you act toward outsiders; **make the most of every opportunity**.*

Noah Webster's 1828 Dictionary gives several definitions for the word *redeem*, including, "to purchase back, to ransom, to rescue, or to recover." To redeem time, Webster says, "is to use more diligence in the improvement of it. To be diligent and active in duty and preparation."

Have you ever been in the middle of a rotten, terrible day, when somebody came along and said the exact thing that you needed to hear, and it redeemed your day? I've experienced that so many times in my life. Right in the middle of what felt like a bad day I've had people speak to me the very thing I needed to hear. It might not have been what I *wanted* to hear, but it was what I *needed* to hear, and my whole attitude was turned around. It "made my day." Words of life were spoken into my heart and lifted my spirit.

I want to be someone who speaks words of life. I want to be one of those people who knows how to redeem the time and make the most of every opportunity to speak good words. So, how do I do that?

How do you "redeem the time"? How do you "make the most of every opportunity"? The next verse in Colossians 4 tells us how:

Let your speech be alway with grace, seasoned with salt, that ye may know how ye ought to answer every man.

Colossians 4:6, KJV

Let your conversation be always full of grace, seasoned with salt, so that you may know how to answer everyone.

Colossians 4:6, NIV

Grace

We are to speak words of grace. Some definitions of grace include "favor, kindness, love, and pardon." Speak words of grace to people. We live in a world where people are harassed and torn apart all day long. They don't need to come to church and get that again. They don't need to call up a Christian friend and get it again. They need grace. They need people who will speak those words of favor, kindness, love, and pardon. Always let your words be words of grace. That's what the Bible says.

Salt

This verse in Colossians 4 goes on to say that our words should be seasoned with salt. What does salt do for you?

Salt makes you thirsty. I want to ask you something. When you speak to people, do you make them thirsty for the Lord? When you speak to lost people or when you speak to Christians, do you leave them more thirsty for Jesus? My friend, contrary to the impression that they might give you, people want Jesus—they just don't always know it. It is our job to have words that are seasoned with salt to make people thirsty. Every time somebody leaves you, they ought to be going, "There is something about that person. He has his act together. I want what he's got." You should make people thirsty.

Salt preserves. Before we had refrigerators, people kept their meat good by packing it in salt. Are you a preserving agency? Are people able to be strong in the Lord because of you? Are your words building up and preserving their faith? Or do people get rotten when they get around you?

Salt seasons. It adds spice; it makes things pleasant. When you taste something that is bland, what do you do?

heart. You are not even trying to live a pure, righteous, and holy life. Do you know what you are doing? You are trampling upon the blood of Jesus. You are purposely, deliberately continuing in your sin. Listen, repentance means more than being sorry. It means turning 180 degrees and going in a different direction. That's repentance. The grace of God is free, but it is not cheap. It cost Jesus' very life. Some of you are treading upon Jesus. You'd better stop it. You'd better be careful. He won't put up with it.

Who is under whose feet? Are you under satan's feet? Is satan under your feet? Is Jesus under your feet?

4. All things will be under Jesus' feet.

If anything is for sure, it is that all things will one day be put underneath Jesus' feet. That means all things. The Scriptures clearly teach us this in First Corinthians 15:24-27:

Then the end will come, when He hands over the kingdom to God the Father after He has destroyed all dominion, authority and power.

*For **He** must reign until **He has put all His enemies under His feet.***

The last enemy to be destroyed is death.

*For **He** "**has put everything under His feet**...."*

Philippians 2:9-11 is one of my favorite portions of Scripture. I love these verses.

Therefore God exalted Him to the highest place and gave Him the name that is above every name,

*that at the **name of Jesus every knee should bow,** in heaven and on earth and under the earth,*

*and every tongue confess that Jesus Christ is Lord, to
the glory of God the Father.*

I can't wait until that coronation day when time is no
more. Every knee will bow and every tongue will confess
that Jesus Christ is Lord. Every person who has ever lived
is going to fall on his or her knees helplessly before the
King of kings, raise his or her hands, and publicly pro-
claim before all the witnesses—the heavenly hosts, all the
saints, and all of mankind from the beginning—Jesus
Christ as Lord.

I believe that after each person stands one by one before
the Lord, he or she will be either welcomed into the
Kingdom or sadly ushered away to hell. How sad it will be
to hear Jesus say things like, "Father, I gave Susie chance
after chance after chance to serve Me. She was ashamed of
Me. She would never surrender and commit her life to Me.
Father, I don't know her." At that moment I believe some of
the angels will sadly but firmly usher the person away into
the outer darkness.

I even believe that, after every individual and all the
heavenly host has stood before the King of kings and the
Lord of lords, all the demonic forces will be brought before
the throne of God to confess that "Jesus is Lord!" And finally, I believe that lucifer himself will have to come and fall
down on his knees before the King of kings and say, "Jesus
Christ is Lord." I can't wait until that day!

Friend, who is under whose feet in your life? Are you
under satan's feet? Are you his puppet? Does he toy with you?

Does he torment you? Are you in the clutches of and under the power of satan? Some of you are so depressed and feel so hopeless. Maybe you laugh and put on a smile in public, but even when you are laughing, you are so miserable inside.

Or is satan under your feet? Are you walking in the authority that God has called you to walk in?

Are you treading upon the blood of Jesus? Is Jesus under your feet? Woe to you if Jesus is under your feet. Let me tell you something, and I want to make myself clear here on this point. Young people, when the Holy Spirit is dealing with you, I want you to run. Run to your bedside and fall on your knees. Run to the altar at church. Respond when the Holy Ghost is dealing with you.

Or, are you under the feet of Jesus? Have you submitted yourself to Jesus Christ as your Savior and Lord in every area of your life? If not, you can do so right now.

The Scriptures teach in Matthew 21:44 that "he who falls on this stone will be broken to pieces, but he on whom it falls will be crushed." Young people, you have a chance right now to fall on your knees, broken before the Lord Jesus Christ, and ask Him to forgive you. But if you refuse to swallow your pride and surrender to Him, there is a day coming when the stone, the rock, Jesus Christ, will fall on you and you will be crushed. You will be destroyed. You will be in eternal hopelessness.

If you are under Jesus' feet, He will make sure that the devil is under your feet.

Again I ask you, who is under whose feet in your life? Here's the good news: If you are under Jesus' feet, He will make sure that the devil is under your feet. If you will put yourself under Jesus' feet, if you will humble yourself, He will exalt you and will put the devil under your feet. He will put that sin out of your life. He will destroy and break the power of that sin over your life.

Right now, as the Holy Spirit is dealing with you, you know that you need to make a decision. You know that there are things in your life that you have got to surrender to the Lord Jesus Christ. When you get serious with God, He'll get serious with you.

I want you, in your own words, to cry out to the Lord. Here is a prayer to get you started:

Holy Spirit, thank You for speaking to my heart; thank You for convicting me of the sin in my life. Thank You for not giving up on me. Lord, I confess my sin and ask that You forgive me. I ask that You deliver me from under the foot of the enemy, and Lord, that You would bring me humbly beneath Your feet. I bow before You and ask You to cleanse me. I ask You to give me a new heart to serve You, Lord. Come into my life in a new way; be my Savior, my Lord, and my Best Friend. I commit my life to You. I want to serve You all the days of my life. In Jesus' name, amen.

C h a p t e r 5

What Time Is It?

It's the last few minutes of the game, and things are getting intense. People are sitting on the edges of their seats. Every play counts. All of a sudden everybody in the stands is going bananas. They are screaming, "Go! Go! Go!" The announcer is shouting, "This could make or break the game right here. This could be the back breaker. This could be it!" Then the fans are screaming so loudly you can't even hear the announcer anymore. They are going bananas.

You get the picture. Now, if you were to act that way at the very beginning of the game; if you were jumping up and down and screaming, "Go! Go, kill 'em!" everybody around you would turn and say, "Uh-oh, a weirdo. We sat in the wrong place." They would look at you like you were a lunatic, wouldn't they? You just don't act like that at the beginning of a game. But when it gets down to the final moments, everything is intensified and every play counts. Things start picking up. Let me tell you something. There are several things we can learn about the times we are living in from what happens at the end of a sports event.

1. Every play counts.

Listen to me. We are in the endtimes. Jesus Christ could come back at any moment, and every play counts. Every day of your life counts. Every school period that you sit in counts. It may be the last one. We have got to stir ourselves, shake ourselves, and awaken ourselves and recognize that we are not at the beginning of the ball game. We are at the end, and we have got to make every effort to make every play count for the Kingdom of God. We must take advantage of every opportunity that we have to share the gospel of Jesus Christ with our friends, because the final buzzer (the trumpet—see 1 Thess. 4:16) is about to sound, and then it will be too late!

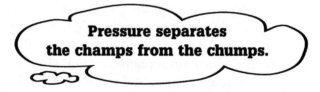

Pressure separates the champs from the chumps.

2. As the pressure of the game intensifies, it separates the champs from the chumps.

Let me tell you something. When the power of God fell on our youth group here in Pensacola, there came a great division between the champs and the chumps. And I'm happy to tell you that the chumps are no more. All I've got now is champs.

Let's look at basketball for a minute. It's the last play of the game—only three seconds are left on the clock. The Chicago Bulls are down one point against some other team. Who's going to get the ball? Michael Jordan is going to get the ball. Why? Because under pressure it's Michael Jordan who wants the ball. He wants to take that shot. Why?

Because at the end of the game when the pressure is on, the chumps collapse and the champs emerge.

Some of you think that it is hard to serve God. If you feel that way, then, friend, you don't serve the same God I serve. My God says in First John 5:3 that His commandments are not grievous; His commands are not burdensome or heavy. If you are finding it hard to serve God, then you are trying to serve Him in your own strength. When you have an intimate relationship with Jesus Christ and you are drawing strength from Him, then it is not a hard thing to serve the Lord. Rather, it is a joy and a pleasure.

When you love somebody, it is not hard to serve that person.

I'll never forget the story I heard of a little ten-year-old girl who was carrying her nine-year-old brother. This boy was bigger than his older sister, but when he fell and scraped his knee, the sister carried him home. An old man came up to the girl and said, "Young lady, put that boy down! He's too big for you." The little girl responded, "No, sir, he's not too big for me. He's my brother." When you love somebody, it is not hard to serve him.

My friend, if you think it is hard to serve God today, go ahead and bail out. What are your options anyway? Bail out. But let me tell you something: If you can't serve Him today, you are never going to make it a month from now. As the time gets shorter, it is going to get more and more intense. Things are going to get even hotter. The pressure is going to get heavier. That's why the Kingdom of God is not for wimps. Many people don't serve God because they are too wimpy. They don't have the backbone to stand up for Jesus. They think that they are big, bad, and tough because they drink, smoke dope, and jump in bed. Listen, anybody can drink, smoke, and jump in bed; but it takes a real man or a real woman to stand up for Jesus Christ and for righteousness.

> **God will use His best available players.**

3. **In the final moments of a game, the coach always puts in his best available players.**

I like this point right here. The coach doesn't put the second string in at the end. He puts his best available players in the game. Notice what I said. The best *available* players, because sometimes his best players aren't available. Do you know why? Sometimes those best players have fouled out of the game. Listen to me. Do you think you can play around with sin? The Bible says that your sin will find you out (see Num. 32:23). If you play around with sin, you are going to be disqualified. You won't have the joy of victory. Sin will bring destruction and ruin to your life.

Let me tell you something, young people. God is not looking for talent or ability; He is looking for *availability*. Take me, for instance. This boy right here doesn't have any talents. All I do is love God and love teenagers. That's all it takes. God is looking for the best available players.

> **God is not looking for ability; He is looking for availability.**

God has handpicked you. When He looked down through the history of time, He saw you.

*For He **chose us in Him before the creation of the world** to be holy and blameless in His sight. In love...*

*He **predestined us** to be adopted as His sons through Jesus Christ, in accordance with His pleasure and will.*

Ephesians 1:4-5

*In Him we were also **chosen,** having been **predestined** according to the plan of Him who works out everything in conformity with the purpose of His will.*

Ephesians 1:11

God knew you before the very foundation of the world was made. I believe that when God was selecting people to live during certain periods of time, He said, "I want these people to live at the beginning of time. I want these people to live during Jeremiah's time. I want these people to live during the time Jesus walked on earth. I want these people to live at the birth of America. And I want *these* people to live in the last times because these are My best. These are My best players; they have warrior hearts."

God is looking for heart. He is looking for those people who will dive after the ball. He is looking for those who will jump higher and run harder. Why? He wants *heart*, not ability. As God looked through the corridors of time, He said, "I want this one to live during the Old Testament. I want this one to live during Jesus' day. I want this one to live in the 1800's. And I want to save My best for the last battle because at the end I will need My greatest warriors." God is raising up a generation of His best for this last day.

4. The coach saves his time-outs for the end of the game.

Did you ever notice that? The coach doesn't use all of his time-outs at the beginning of the game; he saves them for the end. My wife, Jane, goes bananas because I love to watch basketball and she will come into the room and ask, "How many minutes are left?" *Ten minutes.* Then she will come back later and say, "How many minutes are left?" *Six minutes.* Then she will come back, "Now how many minutes are left?" *Three minutes.* This keeps going on, and I keep answering her: *Two minutes. A minute and 45 seconds. A minute. Thirty seconds.* Later she comes in and sees the game still on the screen. "You mean the game is not over yet?!" *No, there are still 23 seconds, sweetheart.* Why does this happen? The coach saved all his time-outs for the end of the game. Why? Because every play is important and he wants to pull players out of the game for a few seconds and give them a pep talk.

Listen to me. In these final days you had better learn how to take time-outs with Jesus. You'd better learn how to pull out of the battle to hear from Him. You'd better learn to come aside with the Coach every day and say, "Okay, God, what is the game plan for today?" If you don't take time-outs with Jesus, you are going to go out there and you are going to get your hiney kicked.

What Time Is It?

We are in a very crucial time in world history, and we need to be aware of it. Look at what Jesus said in Matthew 16:2-3:

> *He replied, "When evening comes, you say, 'It will be fair weather, for the sky is red,'*

> *"and in the morning, 'Today it will be stormy, for the sky is red and overcast.' You know how to interpret*

the appearance of the sky, but you cannot interpret the signs of the times."

Young people, it is very important that we understand the time that we live in. We live in a very crucial time. There are four things about this time that I want us to recognize.

1. It is the WORST time to be alive.

What a sobering thought. Many of you have studied human history. You have studied different time periods and you know that there have been some wicked and dark times. In fact, some of them are even referred to as the Dark Ages. But I want you to understand something: There has never been a day in human history more wicked than the day in which we live today. It's the truth. The apostle Paul warns us in Second Timothy chapter 3 verses 1 through 5:

*But mark this: There will be **terrible times** in the last days.*

People will be lovers of themselves, lovers of money, boastful, proud, abusive, disobedient to their parents, ungrateful, unholy,

without love, unforgiving, slanderous, without self-control, brutal, not lovers of the good,

treacherous, rash, conceited, lovers of pleasure rather than lovers of God—

*having a **form of godliness but denying its power.** Have nothing to do with them.*

People are ungrateful. They are unholy. They are without love. Let me tell you one of the greatest ways to grow your youth group: Love people. Don't be one of those youth groups where somebody comes, visits, and then leaves, saying, "These are the biggest bunch of snobs in town." My goal for Brownsville's youth group is for them to love people unconditionally.

I remember one specific youth service when two young, strong teenage guys came in and people were greeting them and hugging on them. After about ten minutes, they had endured all they could handle and those boys went running out the door. Someone asked them why they were leaving and they said, "We just can't handle all this love and hugging stuff." But you know what? Three weeks later they were back. This generation is hungry for real people who really care.

People these days are not lovers of good. They are treacherous. They are rash. They are conceited. They are lovers of pleasure more than lovers of God. Let me tell you something, young people. I think that God is sick and tired of youth groups who just want to have fun. He is sick and tired of youth groups who just want pizza parties and volleyball. He is sick and tired of young people who are going after pleasure more than they are going after God. Friend, don't be one of those young people who are the first ones to sign up for a lock-in, but who always have something else to do when there's a prayer meeting.

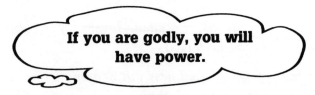

If you are godly, you will have power.

Second Timothy 3:5 speaks of people who have a form of godliness, but who deny the power. We are to have nothing to do with such people. Let me tell you something. You may think that you are a godly, holy person, but if you don't have the power of God working through your life, you are not godly. You might have a form of godliness; you might look good on the outside, but if there is sin in your life, you will not have the power of God.

In this day and age it doesn't take the intelligence of a rocket scientist to know that there are many people reading this book who are already hooked on pornography. Many of you are already hooked on lust. Listen, one of the most damnable things you can do is put a TV in your bedroom. You want to live for God, but you go to your bedroom and the next thing you know, you are flipping through channels and watching stuff you shouldn't be watching. You are entertaining lustful thoughts and you can't understand why you aren't a strong Christian. God is calling for holiness in this generation. We can scream and shout about the power, but friend, we need to have more than a form of godliness. We need to have the real thing.

Having only a form of godliness was certainly the problem with the Church up until recently, but now the Lord is returning the power. The power of God is what will draw people. The power of God is what will set them free.

> **The power of God is what will draw people; and the power of God is what will set them free.**

I'll never forget one of the most amazing things I've ever experienced in this revival. One Thursday night three kids came to our youth meeting. They didn't even believe in God—they were atheists. The only reason they came to the meeting was because one of my young people kept pestering them to come. So in walked these two guys and a young lady. One of the guys came in on crutches. All three of them were about 18 or 19 years old. They sat through our praise and worship and all the way through my preaching. They sat all the way through the altar call and watched at the end as we prayed for young people. God was just wiping people out that night; they were shaking, falling, and jerking.

These three atheists were sitting in the back and making fun of the Holy Ghost. That's dangerous. They were sitting in their seats going, "Ha ha," and doing all these weird things to make fun of what God was doing. All of a sudden, the girl came leaping and jumping over the bodies of people on the floor, people who had been "zapped by God." She was crying uncontrollably. Her face was red and she was calling out, "Mister! Mister!" She didn't know who I was; she just knew that I was up front and that I seemed to be in charge. I turned to her and said, "What is it?" She said, "You won't believe what has just happened!" I said, "What?" For a minute I wondered if God had slapped them around or something because of their mocking attitudes. She said, "We were making fun of you guys and all of a sudden God healed my friend's knee!"

I was stunned. "What?!" I was so surprised. I didn't know that God did stuff like that for atheists and people who make fun of Him. I ran over and there was this 19-year-old, strong, good-looking fellow who five minutes earlier thought he was a big hot shot; and now he was sobbing like a baby and running up and down the stairs to the balcony. I said, "What just happened to you?" He just kept running up and down the stairs crying out how God had healed him. Needless to say, those three teenagers are not atheists anymore.

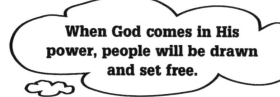

When God comes in His power, people will be drawn and set free. *Lord, come in Your power!* We live in such a wicked day. We live in the worst time to be alive. Crime is rampant all across our land. On a daily basis we hear about murders—hideous murders, like mothers killing their children. We are talking about mothers killing their children—strapping their children in the backseat and pushing the car into the lake. We are talking about mothers taking tiny babies, who are crying and won't stop, and banging their little heads against the wall until they are dead.

These are hideous times we live in. We constantly read about wickedness in the papers. Every day we see drug busts. Young people are bound to drugs. They are trying to escape the pain that is in their lives through drugs, hallucinations, and alcohol. Every day we read in the newspaper about alcohol-related deaths. Teenage pregnancy is constantly escalating, and abortion goes right along with it. We live in a very wicked day. We see this so often that we are numb to it. We can see it and not even be moved. Every once in a while we might know somebody personally and we go, "Oh." But then it is right back to normal again. Sin is such a rampant thing in America that we are no longer moved.

Our homes are being destroyed by divorce. Many of you, probably 50 percent, are victims of divorce yourself. It is a wicked day in which we live. Our schools are falling apart. Many of you go to school fearful because you know the trash that is there. You know people who carry guns and knives. You know people who smoke joints, who shoot up, or who take pills between classes. There are places in your school where you are afraid to go because you are scared that you might get jumped on and somebody might beat the living daylights out of you just for a couple of bucks. We live in a very wicked world. People are overwhelmed with feelings of hopelessness.

Just recently I read about a young man who stood up in a speech class. It was his turn to give a speech, and as he stood up in front of the entire class he asked this question: "What is the meaning of life?" Nobody said a thing. He turned to his teacher and said, "Teacher, tell me, what is the purpose in life?" She was stunned by the question and didn't answer him. He said, "There is no purpose. There is no hope in life. Life is a big joke." Then he pulled out a gun and shot himself in front of his entire class. Why? Because of the hopelessness that is upon this generation.

We live in a very wicked day, young person. There has never been a time in all of human history where there has been so much perversion, so much wickedness, so much killing, so much hatred, so much destruction as the day in which we live. No wonder suicide among teenagers continues to escalate year by year. Many of your friends look down the road to the future and don't see any reason to live. This is a wicked day, but we should not be surprised. Paul warned us that the last days would be terrible times.

But...

"But." I said, *"But."* Someday I want to preach on the "buts" in the Bible. Whenever the word *but* comes in, everything that was said before doesn't matter. If someone is talking to you and all of a sudden he or she says, "But," you can just go ahead and forget everything that was previously said. "I love you and you are the greatest thing that ever happened to me, but...." Get ready. It is "Dear John" time. "I love you and wouldn't hurt you for anything; you are my best friend, but...." Go ahead and walk away. It is over. When the "but" comes, everything in front of it goes out the window. This is the worst time in history that you can ever live in, *but* in Romans 5:20 (KJV) it says this:

> ...*But* where sin abounded, grace did much more abound.

2. It is the GREATEST time to be alive.

Let me tell you something, young person. It is true that this is the worst day we could ever live in, *but* it is also the greatest day in which we could ever live. This is the greatest time in human history. Look at what God said in Acts chapter 2 verses 17 and 18 (KJV):

> And it shall come to pass **in the last days,** saith God, I will pour out of My Spirit upon all flesh: and your sons and your daughters shall prophesy, and your young men shall see visions, and your old men shall dream dreams:

> And on My servants and on My handmaidens I will pour out **in those days** of My Spirit; and they shall prophesy.

God is never taken by surprise.

Yes, we live in wicked days, but we also live in a time with the greatest opportunities that have ever come to human history. God is never taken by surprise. Hear what I am saying: There are many times when we are caught off guard, and there are many times when satan is caught off guard, but God is never taken by surprise. He knew that the last days were going to be perilous times. He even warned us of it. But He also said that where sin abounds, grace does much more abound. He told us that these last days would be wicked, but He also promised that in the last days He would pour out His Spirit and set the captives free. God is never taken by surprise. Satan can just go ahead and rally his entire forces of hell together, but God will just go "Pooh!" and blow them all off the face of the earth. Listen, the dark and evil days are not going to win. Satan never has been and never will be a match or a threat for God.

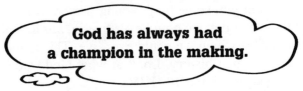

God has always had a champion in the making.

Throughout history, God has always had a champion in the making who, when the time was right, stepped forward and destroyed the powers of darkness. Most of these champions were not recognized until the battle was already won. Think about it.

Noah was one of God's champions. God was about to wipe out the entire earth because it was so wicked. When Noah arrived on the scene, the Bible says that Noah found grace in the eyes of the Lord (see Gen. 6:8 KJV). Noah was a champion of God. Was he ever recognized by his peers? Absolutely not. They called him a fool. They said, "Noah, you're weird. What are you doing building a massive boat?

You are weird. It has never rained before. What are you talking about, Noah?"

Noah just kept preaching repentance. He kept preaching holiness. He kept on preaching judgment. Did people recognize him as a champion? No. Then, after about a hundred years, he finishes the ark and starts getting the animals. People again made fun of him. "What are you doing, creating a zoo? Noah, you are weird, man." Noah was not recognized as a champion until it was too late.

Think of Moses. Did the Israelites accept Moses as a champion? Of course not. Exodus 2:11-14 tells how Moses saw an Egyptian mistreating a slave, so Moses went and killed the Egyptian. The next day one of the Israelites came and said, "Who do you think you are?" Moses ran and hid for about 40 years. The Bible says that he was on the backside of the desert (see Ex. 3:1 KJV). God kept him hidden. God was preparing a champion, but the people didn't recognize who he was until after he began performing great miracles and delivered them from the Egyptians.

Consider David. Did people recognize David as a champion? Absolutely not. David was just a teenage shepherd boy taking lunch to his brothers. He gets to the battlefield and he hears Goliath cursing his God. He says, "Hey guys, isn't somebody going to do something?" His brothers said, "Oh, David, you don't know anything about war. Just go on back to your sheep, you naughty little boy." Nobody recognized David as a great champion until he came back with Goliath's head. Then all of a sudden everybody started singing David's praises.

What about Jesus? Did people recognize Jesus as a great champion? Definitely not. They mocked Him. They called

Him a heretic. They called Him a lunatic. And when He died on the cross, even His own followers hung their heads in shame, thinking it was a most despicable defeat. But three days later when Jesus came forth from the tomb, all of a sudden they recognized Him as King of kings and Lord of lords.

Listen to me. God's champions were never recognized as His champions until they had fought, won the battle, and brought deliverance to His people.

Let me remind you of the words of Paul in First Timothy 4:12a: "Don't let anyone look down on you because you are young." I believe that this generation is a generation from which deliverance will come. God spoke to my heart several years ago from Psalm 24:6 (KJV):

This is the generation of them that seek Him, that seek [His] face....

Society has labeled this generation (those between 15 and 30 years old) as "Generation X." They say that you have no purpose, no goals, and no ambition. They say that we need to cross you off and therefore refer to you as "Generation X." I believe, however, that society has actually spoken prophetically, and *blessed* you with that term. Let me share with you what I believe it could mean.

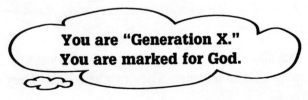

You are "Generation X."
You are marked for God.

1. The letter "X" is the symbol for the Greek letter *chi*, which was often used as an abbreviation for *Christos*, or Christ. I believe that you are "Generation Christ"! Do you know what *Christ* means? It means "Anointed One." I believe that you are the anointed generation that is going to break the curse of sin over our land.

2. The letter "X" is the unknown factor in an algebraic equation that helps you solve the problem and find the solution! I do not believe that you are the problem with America. I believe that you are the only hope America has left!

3. The letter "X" marks the spot where buried treasure is located on a treasure map. The key word here is *buried.* Too often society looks at the teens of today and sees only the pink or purple hair, the body piercings, and the leather. God looks beyond the outer jars of clay and sees the treasure buried inside.

   *But we have this **treasure** in jars of clay to show that this all-surpassing power is from God and not from us.*

   2 Corinthians 4:7

   In my studies of biblical history, I've learned that when a family in Bible times had to travel with expensive jewels, they would place them inside average-looking clay jars so as not to draw attention to them. I believe that there is a gold mine in this generation that will be discovered for the Kingdom of God!

4. Finally, the letter "X" is the symbol in mathematics for multiplication. Recently, we have seen people added to the Kingdom on a daily basis; but

I believe that they will soon be multiplying into the Kingdom because of the champions of this generation! This is a great time to be alive!

Do you remember reading in the Bible about Moses' birth? (See Exodus 1–2.) The devil knew that a deliverer was about to be born and satan wanted to destroy him. Therefore, satan moved upon the government leader of that day, Pharaoh, and had him issue a decree for all the baby boys to be killed. God, however, supernaturally placed His hand upon Moses and spared his life. Moses grew to become the great deliverer of the Old Testament.

Do you remember reading about Jesus' birth? (See Matthew chapter 2.) Again God's people were in bondage. Spiritual darkness had been over the land for more than 400 years. Satan knew that there was another deliverer coming, and once again he moved upon the government leader. King Herod issued a decree that all baby boys in and around Bethlehem were to be killed. God spared Jesus from a premature death, and He became the greatest deliverer of all time!

Listen, young person, a couple of decades ago when your generation was being born, satan once again sensed the timing for a deliverer to come. He moved upon the government leaders of our day and had them issue a decree across America that allowed babies to be killed. Why? Satan knows that this generation is a dangerous generation. This generation is going to put satan in his place. I believe that with all my heart. From this generation will come deliverance. But you see, America doesn't recognize it yet. Just as past champions were not recognized until they had gotten the victory, a lot of people are looking at you and writing you off. They don't recognize you as the champions God has ordained you to be. But I believe that God is about to raise you up and push you to the forefront.

3. *It is the MOST INTENSE time to be alive.*

This is the worst time to live in, and it is the greatest time to live in. Now let's go back to what I talked about at the beginning of this message: This is the most intense time in history to live in. The shorter the time gets, the more intense things become. We have people who come here to Brownsville and constantly ask the question, "Why is the revival so intense?" I'll tell you: It's because we recognize that the time is short.

Friend, we are in the final moments of the game. Every play counts. God is separating the champs from the chumps. He is pulling His best available players to the forefront for this end-time battle. Right now, at this very moment, even as you read this book, you need to take some time out to talk to God. In the heat of the battle is not the time to decide whether or not you are going to be 100 percent committed to God. The time is now.

My friend, do you know Jesus? If you don't know Jesus, or if you are playing games and doing a little religious thing, you are, of all people, most miserable.

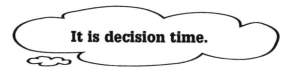

It is decision time.

Deuteronomy chapter 30 verses 19 and 20 say,

*...I have set before you life and death, blessings and curses. Now **choose life**, so that you and your children may live*

and that you may love the Lord your God, listen to His voice, and hold fast to Him....

Listen to me, young person. This is the day of decision. Some of you have grown up in church and have played games. There have been times when you have been hot for God; and there have been times when you've played around with sin, thinking that you could get away with it. Those days are over. You can't switch jerseys and play on different teams anymore. God will not use halfhearted, half-committed soldiers in this war. He is looking for people who will be totally sold out for Him. If you are complacent and wishy-washy, you will be killed in the battle. The Scriptures say that a double-minded man is unstable in all his ways (see Jas. 1:8 KJV). It is time to decide who you are going to serve. God is looking for a generation who will make a bold, radical decision and commitment.

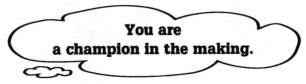

You are a champion in the making.

God has chosen you. He has handpicked and selected you to be born in this generation. You are not an accident or a liability; you are a champion in the making. You were born for such a time as this. Young person, I promise you, if you will get serious with the Lord, He will get serious with you. Your life will count. You will make a difference; you will help bring deliverance to this generation.

Lift your voice to the Lord right now and ask Him to forgive you for your sin and halfheartedness. Ask Him to cleanse you. Ask Him to not pass you by. Ask Him to not eliminate you from the game. Ask Him to fill you with His power so you can fulfill His purpose for your life in this generation.

It's time.

Chapter 6

Close Encounters of the Divine Kind

Have you ever been standing in water and accidentally touched an electrical current? If so, you probably could feel the hair on your body stand straight up. Why? Because you had an encounter with power. This is similar to the spiritual experience described in Job 4:14-15:

Fear and trembling seized me and made all my bones shake.

*A spirit glided past my face, and the **hair on my body stood on end**.*

Any time you come in contact with power, you're going to react. If you don't believe me, just stick your tongue in an electrical socket. I guarantee that you are going to react. When you come in contact with the power of Jesus Christ, the King of kings and Lord of lords, some things are going to happen.

> **Any time you come in contact with power, you're going to react.**

Young person, it is possible for you to go many places and meet many different people and yet have your life unchanged by them. Most people whom you meet will never leave a lasting impression upon you. Every day we meet dozens of people—in the corridors of school, at shopping malls, in restaurants—and the vast majority of them leave us totally unimpressed and totally unchanged. But when you experience a close encounter of the divine kind, things will happen. You will be changed one way or the other.

> **It is impossible to have an encounter with God and not be changed.**

Some of you have grown up in a dangerous lifestyle. You have been living in church all day and sleeping underneath a pew at night. That lifestyle can be dangerous because you hear the gospel day in and day out, week in and week out, and as a result, instead of allowing God's Word to soften your heart, you can allow your heart to harden. Ironically, the same fire that will melt wax will harden clay. It is impossible to come into the presence of God and leave unchanged. Either you are going to leave changed for the good or you are going to leave changed for the bad.

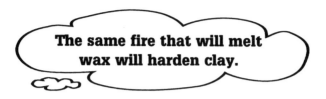

The same fire that will melt
wax will harden clay.

The title of this chapter is "Close Encounters of the Divine Kind." Isaiah chapter 6 tells the story of a divine encounter that Isaiah had with the Lord. As a result of that encounter, Isaiah's life was totally and radically changed.

In the year that King Uzziah died, I saw the Lord seated on a throne, high and exalted, and the train of His robe filled the temple.

Above Him were seraphs, each with six wings: With two wings they covered their faces, with two they covered their feet, and with two they were flying.

And they were calling to one another: "Holy, holy, holy is the Lord Almighty; the whole earth is full of His glory."

*At the sound of their voices the **doorposts and thresholds shook** and the temple was filled with smoke.*

***"Woe to me!"** I cried. "I am ruined! For I am a man of unclean lips, and I live among a people of unclean lips, and my eyes have seen the King, the Lord Almighty."*

Then one of the seraphs flew to me with a live coal in his hand, which he had taken with tongs from the altar.

With it he touched my mouth and said, "See, this has touched your lips; your guilt is taken away and your sin atoned for."

Then I heard the voice of the Lord saying, "Whom shall I send? And who will go for Us?" And I said, "Here am I. Send me!"

Isaiah 6:1-8

In this portion of Scripture we see that Isaiah had an encounter with God. The glory of the Lord filled the temple and the angels cried, "Holy, holy, holy," and all of a sudden the entire place began to shake under the power of God. The very threshold and the pillars began to shake and a glory cloud filled the sanctuary.

If you have hung around revival circles at all, you have probably heard the phrase, "falling out in the Spirit" or "slain in the Spirit." This is nothing new! Revelation 1:17 tells how the apostle John saw the Lord and fell at His feet as if he were dead. Matthew 28:4 (KJV) says that "the keepers did shake, and became as dead men" when an angel came and rolled away the stone from the tomb.

Have you experienced anything like that? I have. Since revival hit us in June of 1995, there have been times here at Brownsville that have blown me away. I remember one night when half of the worship team fell out in the Spirit. The power of God fell in the sanctuary so heavily that sinners began to collapse in the pews. They would fall out as dead men in the aisles and their loved ones would literally pick them up and carry them to the altar.

A meeting of humanity with the glory of God—that is what we should experience regularly in our lives. Three things are exposed when you have an encounter with God:

1. An encounter of the divine kind will expose God's power and glory.

Daniel chapter 10 verses 7 through 11 describe such an encounter.

I, Daniel, was the only one who saw the vision; the men with me did not see it, but such terror overwhelmed them that they fled and hid themselves.

*So I was left alone, gazing at this great vision; **I had no strength left,** my face turned deathly pale and I was helpless.*

*Then I heard him speaking, and as I listened to him, **I fell into a deep sleep, my face to the ground.***

A hand touched me and set me trembling on my hands and knees.

*He said, "Daniel, you who are highly esteemed, consider carefully the words I am about to speak to you, and stand up, for I have now been sent to you." And when he said this to me, I stood up **trembling.***

Verse 8 tells us that when he received the vision, Daniel had no strength left. Have you ever experienced that? When you come into the presence of God, it seems like all your strength just goes out of your body. The Scriptures say that Daniel heard a voice, that he fell into a deep sleep on his face, and that his face was on the ground.

Daniel experienced a manifestation of God. Noah Webster's 1828 Dictionary gives this definition of manifestation: "The act of disclosing what is secret, unseen or obscure; discovery to the eye or to the understanding; the exhibition of any thing by clear evidence." Some people, when looking at the revival here at Brownsville, have questioned and even criticized the manifestations of God's power in our midst. Listen, manifestations are nothing new; there is plenty of recorded evidence. Look for yourself at what went on in some of the revivals throughout history. Look for yourself in the pages of the Bible! When Almighty God shows up around mortal men, there are manifestations of His power!

Daniel fell face down on the ground. He was lying there, prostrate before God, when all of a sudden he felt God pick him up and put him on his hands and knees. Then God told him to stand up, and Daniel stood trembling in the presence of God. I've seen people tremble in this revival. I've seen God pick people up. I've even seen His power throw them against the wall!

Acts 7:30-32 describes what happened to Moses when he saw the flaming fiery bush. Wouldn't you like to see a bush that is on fire but doesn't burn up? When Moses saw it, the wonder of the sight drew him to it. When he got there, the Lord spoke to him, and all of a sudden Moses began to tremble in the presence of God.

In Acts chapter 9 you can read the story of Saul's conversion. A light shone all around him, he fell to the earth, and he heard a voice. Verse 6, in the King James Version, says that Saul was trembling and astonished. The men who were with him were speechless, and Saul was blind for three days. So far we at Brownsville have not seen anyone blinded for three days. People may criticize and wonder, but manifestations here in Pensacola are still mild according to the things that happened in the Bible!

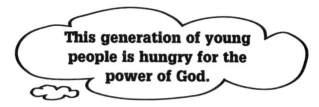

This generation of young people is hungry for the power of God.

God wants to bring an encounter with the Holy Ghost into the Church. He is returning His power and glory to the house of God. You, my friend, are part of a whole generation of young people who are hungry for this to happen.

I remember one Friday night when a group of about six teenagers came to church after a football game at their high school. Some of my guys had finally coerced their friends to check out a revival meeting. I remember noticing them in the overflow area, sitting there with their eyes bugging out. These kids were not used to going to church, especially this kind of church. They had never seen anything like it in their lives.

At the end of the service, when we were praying for people, these teenagers shook their heads and said, "This is weird stuff." One of my young men finally convinced them to come down out of the balcony and at least talk to me. It was about 2:00 a.m. by then. I went up to them and said, "Do you all want me to pray for you?" They shook their heads emphatically, "No."

I found out that these guys were the bullies of the high school and that one of them was especially mean and ornery. One of my young ladies came over and called him by name. Then she said, "I can't believe you! I've never seen you back down from anybody. What's the matter? Are you chicken or something?" What's the poor guy to do? He answered, "I'm not chicken." She said, "Then let me pray for you." He said, "Okay." She reached out her pretty little hand and hardly even got her fingers on his forehead when he fell out in the Spirit.

His five buddies got so scared that they were back up in the balcony before he hit the floor. Twenty minutes later the young man got up and said, "What happened to me?!" and received Jesus Christ as his Lord and Savior.

> **This generation is sick and tired of hearing the old stories of how God used to move years ago. They want God today!**

The reason thousands of people from all over the world are coming to Pensacola, Florida, is because they are hungry for the power of God. This generation is sick and tired of hearing the old stories of how God used to move years ago. They want God today! When you remove power and authority, respect is gone. When power and authority left the Church, respect for the Church left.

Let me give you a case in point. Suppose you are driving along having a good time, listening to the radio, and you look up and see a police car. What do you immediately do? You don't even look to see if you are speeding; you just automatically touch the brake pedal. Why? It is because of the presence of authority. When you see that little blue light come over the crest of the hill, all of a sudden you drive differently. We need God to show up again in the Church. When God comes on the scene, people will start living differently.

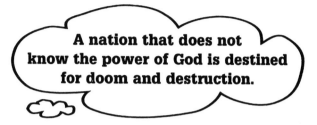

A nation that does not know the power of God is destined for doom and destruction.

America became the greatest nation in the world because it was birthed in the flames of revival. But America turned its back on God and we are now paying the price. A nation that does not know the power of God is destined for doom and destruction. How can a great nation like ours fall headlong into the pit of despair and hopelessness? I'll tell you how: no power.

Why is crime, hideous crime, rampant and rising in America? Because there is no power. Why are hundreds and thousands of teenagers committing suicide every day? Because there is no power. Why are the majority of homes being torn apart by divorce in America? Because there is no power. Why are illegal drugs one of the largest business industries today? Because there is no power. Why are Americans becoming so sexually perverted that there is no longer public shame even for homosexual acts, but they do them publicly? Because there is no power. How can this nation's citizens murder entire generations of children through abortion and use these precious infants to make cosmetics, smearing them on their faces? Because there is no power. We must have the power of God in our churches once again!

2. An encounter of the divine kind will expose sin.

We've been duped. The devil has slowly shut off the lights and now we no longer recognize our sin. When the power is gone and there is no light, do you know what happens? Sin becomes rampant. When you come in contact with the King of kings and the Lord of lords, the light of Jesus Christ will begin to expose your sin.

We live in a very dark world. You, young person, are being taught that there are no absolutes. But I am telling you, as a preacher of the gospel of Jesus Christ, that there is an absolute and it is the Word of God. In secular education, youth are being told that everything is relative. Listen, everything is relative only when it is based upon the Word of God. Where there is darkness, there is no conviction of sin. Why do people go party at night? Why don't they get up in the morning and go party then? Why don't they get up and get drunk first thing in the morning? Why don't they have their illicit sex in the noon day out there for everybody to see? I'll tell you why: The Scriptures say that men love darkness. Look at John 3:19-20:

> *This is the verdict: Light has come into the world, but* **men loved darkness instead of light because their deeds were evil.**
>
> *Everyone who does evil hates the light, and will not come into the light for fear that his deeds will be exposed.*

Young person, you might think that your sin is hidden in darkness, but the Scriptures say, "For nothing is secret, that shall not be made manifest; neither any thing hid, that shall not be known and come abroad" (Lk. 8:17 KJV). There will be a day when all shall be seen. You might get away with it now, but there will come a day when darkness will be no more and God will shine His light upon your sin.

The problem with this generation is that you were born after the power of God left America. All you have known is darkness. If your great-grandparents were to come alive today and see the things that you see on TV, hear the things that you hear on the radio, or read what you read in the newspapers, they would roll over with a heart attack.

If you go into a dimly lit room and stay there long enough, you will begin to think that you can see clearly. My young friend, all you have known is darkness in America. You don't know the glory days of America. You don't know the days in which America used to honor Jesus Christ. Your eyes have been adjusted to the darkness of this world and you do not understand truth as Jesus intended it. You've been duped. You've been lied to by the devil. You've been lied to by society. They say that you can see clearly, but outside of the Word of God you cannot.

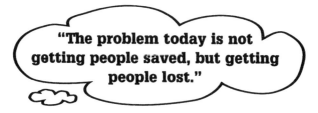

"The problem today is not getting people saved, but getting people lost."

Let me tell you the problem with America today and with countries all around the world. I don't think I could put it any better than James Kennedy when he said, "The problem today is not getting people saved, but getting people lost." Most people don't understand the fact that they are lost. A lot of people think, *I'm okay; I'm as good as the next guy*, because all they know is darkness. Listen, if you do not personally know Jesus Christ as your Lord and Savior, then you are lost.

Recently my family was shopping in a local department store. Caleb, our eight-year-old son, was following my wife Jane and I as we were walking along looking at different items that we needed for our home. Caleb is really excited about fishing right now and, unknown to us, decided to make a little detour to the sporting goods section to look at fishing rods. Jane and I continued walking, then suddenly realized that Caleb was no longer following us. For about 10 or 15 minutes we searched the aisles for our little boy.

Fear hit me. The devil started lying to me and saying, "I have stolen your son. Somebody has picked up your son." A lot of people in Pensacola know me, but at that moment I didn't care what they thought about me. I was going through the store, up and down every hallway and aisle shouting, "Caleb, Caleb, where are you, Caleb?" Caleb was lost.

One of the store attendants saw my face and heard the panic in my voice and she said, "What's the matter, sir?" "My eight-year-old son is missing. I can't find him." They quickly got on the intercom, "Adam alert, Adam alert," and described my son. "Adam alert: eight-year-old boy; brown hair and wearing such and such shirt. Adam alert." That alarm went throughout the entire store and almost every worker dropped what he or she was doing and started looking for my son.

All the while, Caleb was happily engrossed in the sporting goods section. He wasn't even concerned. My son didn't even realize that he was lost. He heard the Adam alert, but he didn't know what it was. He was just contentedly looking at the fishing poles while his father was having a heart attack. "Caleb, Caleb, where are you?!"

Listen to me. There is an "Adam alert" for you, my friend. Genesis 3:8-9 tells how God the Father came down to the Garden of Eden and called, "Adam, where are you?" God is calling to some of you and saying, "I see you are in church, but I want to know, where are you?" Father God has dispatched His Holy Spirit to search the world over for you. He has dispatched His angels and His servants to get hold of your heart. You had better wake up and realize your condition. Recognize that you are lost.

It is hard to get people saved when they don't know that they are lost. But listen, when we encounter the Light; when God begins to turn His searchlights on us, all of a sudden we become like Isaiah and say, "Woe is me; I am unclean."

I was a religious sinner.

I grew up in the Catholic church. In fact, I was an altar boy for ten years. I went to confession properly, I attended every service, and I was in catechism (Sunday school) all my life. But I was a religious sinner. I did not personally know Jesus Christ as my Lord and my Savior. This was not the fault of the Catholic Church; it happens in every denomination. It is very possible to grow up knowing how to "do church," but not know Jesus.

Then Jesus Christ turned the light on me. I was 16 years old at the time, and I decided to visit a little Assembly of God church in my hometown. The Light of Jesus hit me in the pew that night, and all of a sudden I could see clearly. I saw that my religion was not going to do me any good. I saw that I was just a religious sinner going to hell.

I was in the second pew on the right-hand side of that little church. There were approximately 30 people there. I could not tell you today what the evangelist preached on, but I know what God said. He spoke to my heart and said, "Richard, you had better get right with Me, or you are going to split hell wide open." I remember so clearly getting up out of the second pew of that little church, walking down to the front, and kneeling at an old-fashioned altar.

As I mentioned previously, an altar is where your life gets altered. It is much more than confession; it is repentance. It is a change of lifestyle. It is not saying, "God, I'm sorry," and then continuing on with what you were doing. It is, "God, I'm sorry, and with Your help I will never do it again." That night when I went forward to the altar, God radically changed my life. I suddenly understood Second Corinthians 5:17 (KJV):

> *Therefore if any man be in Christ, he is a new creature: old things are passed away; behold, all things are become new.*

When you have a personal encounter of a divine kind, it exposes God's glory, it exposes your sin, and now for our third point…

3. **An encounter of the divine kind exposes God's call on your life.**

When Isaiah saw the Lord, he immediately began to cry out, "God, I am a man of unclean lips. God, I'm a sinful man." When you come into the presence of a holy God, all of a sudden you recognize how unholy you are. The Scriptures are true:

As it is written: "There is no one righteous, not even one...."

Romans 3:10

For all have sinned and fall short of the glory of God.

Romans 3:23

For the wages of sin is death, but the gift of God is eternal life in Christ Jesus our Lord.

Romans 6:23

Immediately after Isaiah repented, saying that he was a man of unclean lips, he heard God call out, "I've got a message, and I'm looking for a messenger." I can just see Isaiah one minute saying, "God, I'm not worthy," and the next minute, "God, if You'll let me, I'll go. I'll do it, God; I'll do it!"

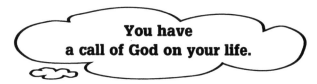

You have a call of God on your life.

I want you to understand something. Every person, including *you*, my friend, has a call of God on his or her life. Some are called to be teachers. Some are called to be godly lawyers and godly politicians. Some are called to be doctors. Some are called to be nurses. Some are called to be housewives. Some are called to be carpenters. Everyone is called to something.

And then there are some who, every time they have an encounter with God, something clicks inside them. Some of you know what I'm talking about. When you have a real encounter from God, something clicks deep inside of you and you go, "God, would You be calling me to full-time ministry?" I know that because I have experienced it.

Growing up as a young Catholic boy, I used to tell my family all the time that I wanted to be a priest someday. I had a great-uncle who was a priest. There was also a nun in my family. Throughout my early childhood, I too wanted to be a man of the cloth. Then, in the sixth grade, something happened to me—I got my first love note from a girl. All of a sudden, I didn't want to be a priest anymore.

My great-grandmother, Mimi, was a godly woman who had a big influence on my life. I remember going to her bedside and listening as she said her rosary, or as she talked to me about the Lord. I remember the last time I saw her. She was in her mid-80's, and I was in the sixth grade. I remember standing beside her bed when she could barely even talk. She grabbed my hand and squeezed it, and said, "Ricky [my family calls me Ricky], are you still going to be a priest?" By this time I had decided that I wasn't; but with her being on her deathbed, I didn't have the heart to tell her no. So I said, "Yes, I'm going to be a priest." Even while I said those words, there was uncertainty in my heart. I didn't want to be a priest anymore, but somewhere deep inside of me was a longing to preach the Word of God.

When I received Jesus Christ as my Savior at age 16, God immediately started dealing with my life. Every time I would have an encounter with Him in the quietness of my prayer time or in a church service, there was something inside me going, "God, I want to be a preacher. God, I want to preach the Word." But I became confused by the mixed messages I heard. I knew preachers who got in the pulpit and said stuff like, "Woe is me if I don't preach the gospel." They made it sound like you shouldn't want to preach. They would say stuff like, "Be sure that you are called. We have too many self-called prophets already." I became so confused as a young man who loved Jesus—all I wanted to do was preach, but I was left feeling like I shouldn't.

I remember when we would have prophets come to the church. They would call out people and say things about their future. I always sat in the front and would practically squeeze my knuckles white on the pew praying, "God, let them call me out and tell me I'm going into the ministry." Not one of them ever called me out. I lived that way for about four years: knowing the Lord, wanting to go into the ministry, yet uncertain of His call on my life.

I did everything in the church that I knew to do. I was a Sunday school teacher and ran a bus route that picked up 50 kids each week. I was in the adult choir and the youth choir, and I did nursing home ministry on the weekends. I was going after God. I was doing everything I could for Jesus. I graduated from Pensacola Junior College with an AA in accounting. I was at the University of West Florida studying to be a Certified Public Accountant because I loved to crunch numbers and I'm good at math. I did not know for sure that God had called me, and I refused to be a self-called prophet, but the desire burned inside me: "God, I wish I could preach."

I'll never forget January 18, 1982, at 2:00 in the morning. I could take you to the spot. I was working at that time in the hospital and going to school at night. I had come home, finished my homework, and was doing my devotions as I always do before I go to bed. I could take you to the red beanbag that I was sitting in. That's when God tapped me on the shoulder. He didn't speak to me in an audible voice, but He said, "Richard, it is time to go into full-time ministry."

I remember feeling so scared. Listen to me. I am speaking to some of your hearts right now. Some of you know exactly where I was at because you feel that same way. I was so scared.

Now, you've got to understand something. I was one of the few Criscos who had ever graduated from high school at that time. All my life my parents told me, "Richard, you are going to be a doctor or lawyer or accountant. You are going to be someone who makes money." They pushed me in school. I made almost straight A's at school, and I had to work hard for every one of my grades. If you were one of those people who never studied and still made A's, I hated you. I was so excited when you missed a question and I got it right. I had to work for everything. I had worked and worked and my parents had pushed and pushed, and now I was going to have to go to my mom and dad and tell them that I wasn't going to be an accountant. That was a scary thought. My parents were already upset with me because I had left the Catholic Church. My parents are true Catholics. In fact, they still go to the Catholic Church today, while they also come to revival services at Brownsville. They love Jesus.

My parents were already upset with me for leaving the Catholic Church. Now I was going to turn around and tell them that I wasn't going to go back to school; I was going to go into the ministry. I was scared to death. I'll never forget the night I told them. I sat there at the dinner table, unable to eat, and finally my dad, who is a very stern man, said, "Son, what's the matter?" They could tell there was something wrong with me. I said, "Dad, I've got something

I have to tell you. I'm not going back to school to study to be an accountant. I'm going into the ministry."

His response caught me totally off guard. He said, "I know that." I said, "What?!" My dad went on to tell me how my family had felt that I would be used in the priesthood, especially because of my godly great-grandmother Mimi, and her brother, my great-uncle, Father Vosburgh. My mouth dropped even wider. "Dad, nobody ever told me that before!" He said, "No, we wanted you to go into the ministry because God called you, not because somebody else said that you would."

I was mad. I went and told my pastor what God had spoken to me, and he said, "I know." I said, "Why didn't you tell me?" Why had everybody just left me to wonder and feel confused? Then Morris Cerillo held meetings in a Pensacola church. More than 2,000 people were in the auditorium. When I came through the prayer line, Brother Cerillo had someone tell me to wait off to the side. When he got through praying for everybody, he came back to me and said, "Young man, I don't know if you know this, but God has a call upon your life." I thought, *Why couldn't God tell me this before, when I was asking for it!?* Now I know why. Prophecy should never direct; it should confirm.

Later, when I was a student at Southeastern Bible College, I attended a ministers' meeting to which the students were invited. Dr. Cho, who is pastor of the world's largest church, was the speaker. (Dr. Cho, by the way, prophesied about the revival here in Pensacola in 1993, two years before it happened.) More than a thousand pastors and ministers attended, and on the last night, Dr. Cho was laying hands upon people and praying for them. When he came to me in the prayer line, he asked someone to have me stand off to the side; he wanted to talk to me. Dr. Cho got through praying for all those ministers and then he came over to me. He said, "I don't know if you realize this or not, but God has His hand upon you in a very special way." It is so awesome to think how, years later, the prophecy that he spoke over me and the prophecy that he spoke about the Pensacola revival have come together.

> **If God can create the universe out of nothing, then He can use you.**

Listen, I am just average "Joe Blow Nobody." I haven't told you these things about my life to be proud or boastful. I am telling them to you to give you hope. You might feel like you are an average "Joe Blow Nobody" too. "God, how could You ever use me in ministry?" Maybe you've had people put you down and your confidence in being able to do anything for God has been destroyed. I am telling you right now that if God can create the universe out of nothing, then He can use you. I'm going to tell you something else: There are a lot of people God can't use because they think that they are somebody. God can use only those people who recognize that they are nobodies and He alone is Somebody.

> **God can use only those people who recognize that they are nobodies and He alone is Somebody.**

You may have been desperately wondering what God has for your life. Maybe you are saying, "God, I want to be in the ministry," but you are so afraid to step out because you are not sure it is God's will. I believe the will of God is as simple as Psalm 37:4:

Delight yourself in the Lord and **He will give you** *the desires of your heart.*

Do you know what that Scripture means? It means you are to go after God, young person. Delight yourself in Jesus. Don't worry about tomorrow. Just do today what God wants you to do today. God knows why He created you; He knows your purpose in life. Let me tell you what will happen: As you go after Him, God will take His will and He'll put it inside your heart as a desire. He will *give* you desires that line up to His will.

I believe that the will of God is just that simple. We have overcomplicated it. God knows that we are simple people trying to get in touch with an awesome God. He's not up there with some magical puzzle, laughing at us while we try to figure it out. God is not that way. He wants you to know His will for your life. And it is this simple: Go after God with all your heart. That's the key right there. Go after God with all your heart—then do what you want to do.

> **Go after God with all your heart—then do what you want to do.**

That sounds so contrary to what we have heard many times in church. But I'm telling you what the Bible says. If you will go after God with all your heart, He'll put His will inside you in the form of a desire and then you will do a good job at it. I'm not the best youth pastor in the world, but

I am very good—and I'll tell you the reason why. It's because I love my work. I am doing what God called me to do. I love young people. I love preaching. Listen, you are not going to be good at anything you don't love to do.

Three things happen when you have a close encounter of the divine kind. An encounter with Jesus Christ exposes God's power and glory, it exposes your sin, and it exposes His call upon your life. Some of you have already had your sin exposed by His Light and you have dealt with it. There are others of you who want to do something for God, but you have sin in your life. You can't have God and your sin at the same time. You just can't have both. You can't hold on to the world and hold on to God. You are either friends with the world or friends with God. You cannot be friends of both. You've got to choose.

God's Light is shining down upon you right now. You've got to make a decision. Are you going to hold on to your sin or are you going to let loose and hold on to the hand of God? You need to repent of your sin. Here is a sample prayer for you:

> **God, I'm sick and tired of my sinful ways. I want You to change my heart and my life. Dear Jesus, thank You for turning Your Light on in my soul. Thank You for exposing my sin. I ask You now not only to forgive me but also to change me. Lord, I need heart surgery. I've got a stony heart, a sinful heart, and I need a heart that goes after God. Jesus, create in me a new heart. Renew a right spirit within me. Cast me not away from Your presence, Lord.**

Jesus, I receive You as my Savior, as my Lord, and as my Best Friend. From this day forward You can count on me. I'll be Your friend. I'll bring You glory. I'll bring You honor. And when I stumble, I'll be quick to repent. In Jesus' name, amen.

Some of you might feel that God has clarified the fact that you are called to full-time preaching ministry. That doesn't mean that you are better than anybody else. Just because you say, "I'll preach the gospel," doesn't make you better than the carpenter who hammers nails. I know carpenters who are better Christians than preachers. I'm asking you to forsake all and follow Jesus. Jesus said that He didn't have a pillow to put His head upon (see Lk. 9:58). Jesus said that if you want to follow Him, you have to die with Him (see Lk. 9:23-24).

Young person, if every time you have an encounter with God, something burns inside you about preaching the Word, let me tell you what that something is. It is the Holy Ghost and it is real. I don't care what kind of gifts you have or don't have; don't let that scare you. You might say that you can't do anything, that you don't have a gift in the world. Listen, I'm glad that I'm not gifted at anything. Too many gifted people fall back on their gifts and then they end up flat on their faces. Remember, God uses somebody who knows he or she is nobody. That's the kind of person God looks for.

Here's what someone once told me: If God has called you to full-time ministry, don't ever stoop so low as to become the president of the United States. That saying has never left my heart. God is looking for people who will boldly answer the call, who will respond like Isaiah, "Here I am. Lord, send me."

> **If God has called you to full-time ministry, don't ever stoop so low as to become the president of the United States.**

Let me pray for you...

Dear Jesus, I pray that the words of this chapter will burn within the hearts of everyone who reads them. I pray that each person will have an encounter of the divine kind—a life-changing encounter with Your Holy Spirit. I ask You, Lord, to ignite Your purpose and passion within their lives. May they be consumed by Your call and destiny. May they faithfully fulfill Your purpose for them, whatever that may be. I ask this for Your glory and honor. In Jesus' name, amen.

C h a p t e r   7

No Compromise

As a soldier in Vietnam, Dave Roever was part of a small group that had been specially trained to go ahead of the other soldiers and make initial attacks. Once, when he was on such a mission, Dave was holding a white phosphorus hand grenade. He pulled the pin and was about to throw it in among some snipers when, suddenly, the snipers shot the hand grenade and it exploded in Dave's face. Forty percent of his body was burned and one side of his face was completely gone. His face is totally disfigured.

I have heard Dave, an incredible man of God, share how the Vietnamese knew that we Americans are lazy people; we always take the path of least resistance. So the Vietnamese would set up booby traps where all the trails were at, and we dumb Americans would say, "There's a trail—that's the easy way." We would go through and get our bodies blown apart. Finally the military caught on and trained the soldiers to find the thickest place of the jungle and to beat a path through that spot, because that was the safest way to go.

Young person, I'm telling you right now that if you expect to serve Jesus Christ as your Savior and your Lord, it is not going to be an easy path. Don't expect to be popular at school if you want to be a true Christian for Jesus. I'm talking about a true Christian. A true Christian is going to be constantly cutting vines, knocking down trees, and working for every inch of ground that he or she possesses.

> **The path of least resistance is what makes rivers and men crooked.**

You must climb in order to get to a higher place. You never coast uphill. Many of you want to do great things for God. If you are ever going to do anything great for God, it will cost you. You are going to have to crawl and work for everything that you get in Christ Jesus. The path of least resistance is what makes rivers and men crooked.

In this message, we are going to look at a man who insisted on taking the easy way. His story is in the Book of Genesis, chapter 19.

> *The two angels arrived at Sodom in the evening, and Lot was sitting in the gateway of the city. When he saw them, he got up to meet them and bowed down with his face to the ground.*

> *"My lords," he said, "please turn aside to your servant's house. You can wash your feet and spend the*

*night and then go on your way early in the morning."
"No," they answered, "we will spend the night in the square."*

But he insisted so strongly that they did go with him and entered his house. He prepared a meal for them, baking bread without yeast, and they ate.

Before they had gone to bed, all the men from every part of the city of Sodom—both young and old— surrounded the house.

They called to Lot, "Where are the men who came to you tonight? Bring them out to us so that we can have sex with them."

What a sick generation. Men calling for men to come out so that they can have sex with them.

Lot went outside to meet them and shut the door behind him

and said, "No, my friends. Don't do this wicked thing.

"Look, I have two daughters who have never slept with a man. Let me bring them out to you, and you can do what you like with them. But don't do any- thing to these men, for they have come under the pro- tection of my roof."

"Get out of our way," they replied. And they said, "This fellow came here as an alien, and now he wants to play the judge! We'll treat you worse than them." They kept bringing pressure on Lot and moved forward to break down the door.

But the men inside reached out and pulled Lot back into the house and shut the door.

Then they struck the men who were at the door of the house, young and old, with blindness so that they could not find the door.

The two men said to Lot, "Do you have anyone else here—sons-in-law, sons or daughters, or anyone else in the city who belongs to you? Get them out of here,

"because we are going to destroy this place. The outcry to the Lord against its people is so great that He has sent us to destroy it."

So Lot went out and spoke to his sons-in-law, who were pledged to be married to his daughters. He said, "Hurry and get out of this place, because the Lord is about to destroy the city!" But his sons-in-law thought he was joking.

With the coming of dawn, the angels urged Lot, saying, "Hurry! Take your wife and your two daughters who are here, or you will be swept away when the city is punished."

When he hesitated, the men grasped his hand and the hands of his wife and of his two daughters and led them safely out of the city, for the Lord was merciful to them.

As soon as they had brought them out, one of them said, "Flee for your lives! Don't look back, and don't stop anywhere in the plain! Flee to the mountains or you will be swept away!"

But Lot said to them, "No, my lords, please!

"Your servant has found favor in your eyes, and you have shown great kindness to me in sparing my life. But I can't flee to the mountains; this disaster will overtake me, and I'll die. Look, here is a town near enough to run to, and it is small. Let me flee to it—it is very small, isn't it? Then my life will be spared."

He said to him, "Very well, I will grant this request too; I will not overthrow the town you speak of.

"But flee there quickly, because I cannot do anything until you reach it." (That is why the town was called Zoar.) [Zoar means small or tiny.]

By the time Lot reached Zoar, the sun had risen over the land.

Then the Lord rained down burning sulfur on Sodom and Gomorrah—from the Lord out of the heavens.

Thus He overthrew those cities and the entire plain, including all those living in the cities—and also the vegetation in the land.

But Lot's wife looked back, and she became a pillar of salt.

Early the next morning Abraham got up and returned to the place where he had stood before the Lord.

He looked down toward Sodom and Gomorrah, toward all the land of the plain, and he saw dense smoke rising from the land, like smoke from a furnace.

So when God destroyed the cities of the plain, He remembered Abraham, and He brought Lot out of the catastrophe that overthrew the cities where Lot had lived.

This message is entitled, "No Compromise." Earlier in the Book of Genesis you can read about how Lot and Abraham used to travel together. Abraham was a godly man, and Lot was his nephew. In chapter 13 it tells how their cattle and their possessions multiplied to such a great degree that the land could no longer support them both. When they each went their separate ways, Abraham gave Lot the first choice of the land. Lot considered his options, and chose what appeared to be the easy way.

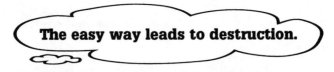

The easy way leads to destruction.

Young person, beware. I want you to understand something about life, now, while you are young. Anything that is worth having will cost you something. It will cost you some energy. It will cost you some sweat. It will cost you some tears. It will cost you some of your life. The easy way leads to destruction (see Prov. 14:12).

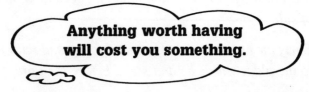

Anything worth having will cost you something.

What is free is not worth having. You might say, "Wait a minute, Brother Richard! Salvation is free." *No. Salvation is not free.* First of all, Jesus Christ gave His life for your salvation; He paid the price. And not only did He pay His life, but salvation will also cost you your own life.

The price is your life.

We have preached a false gospel in America. Jesus said that if anyone wanted to be one of His disciples, he would have to take up his cross and follow Him (see Lk. 9:23). What was He saying? Die. That is what He was saying. The price you must pay to be a true follower of Jesus is your life.

In Matthew 7:13-14, Jesus said,

Enter through the narrow gate. For wide is the gate and broad is the road that leads to destruction, and many enter through it.

But small is the gate and narrow the road that leads to life, and only a few find it.

It is the straight and narrow way that I, Richard Crisco, am looking for. I am willing to take the hard way. Philippians 3:12 is an incredible portion of Scripture. It says,

*Not that I have already obtained all this, or have already been made perfect, but **I press on to take hold** of that for which Christ Jesus took hold of me.*

I want to ask you something, young person. Why did God get a hold of your life? "I don't know. I guess 'cause He loved me." Yes, He loves you. But He had a reason for getting a hold of your life. Some of you think that you got saved just so you could go to Heaven. If that was the case, then God should hurry up and take you there before satan tries to drag you back into sin!

Listen, God didn't save you just so you could go to Heaven; He saved you for a purpose. Yes, we are on our way to Heaven, and I personally can't wait to get there, but there is something for me to do now. There is something for you to do now. Paul said that he was pressing forward to get a hold of that thing, that purpose, for which God had gotten a hold of him. There is a reason why God has gotten hold of your life. Find out what it is and go for it.

I love the next verses, Philippians 3:13 and 14:

*Brothers, I do not consider myself yet to have taken hold of it. But one thing I do: Forgetting what is behind and **straining** toward what is ahead,*

***I press on toward the goal** to win the prize for which God has called me heavenward in Christ Jesus.*

My Brownsville teens have been in revival for three years. I am constantly after them about not getting hung up on what God did yesterday. I tell them not to be "has beens." Here in Philippians 3:13, Paul talks about straining toward what is ahead. I love that word, *straining*. Have you ever watched a 100-yard dasher? That runner is straining and pushing forward with everything that is within him or her.

I want to be like that. I want to keep straining toward what is ahead. I'm pressing on toward the goal to win the prize for which God has called me heavenward in Christ Jesus. There is a straining. There is a pushing. Don't go for the path of least resistance; that's where Lot made his mistake. Lot chose the easy way.

Look back at Genesis 13. When they split up and went their ways, Abraham gave Lot the first choice. He said, "Lot, which way do you want to go?" Lot looked and saw that the land was easy over to the one side. He saw that there was a lot of grass and that it would be easy to take care of his cattle. He wouldn't have to work very hard. He said, "I'll go this direction." Look at verse 12:

Abram [Abraham] *lived in the land of Canaan, while Lot lived among the cities of the plain and* **pitched his tents near Sodom.**

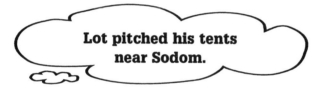

Lot pitched his tents near Sodom.

In my Bible, I have underlined the word, *near.* That's where Lot made a big mistake—he started to hang out near sin.

I get so concerned about young people who ask me if it is all right for them to participate in a questionable activity. "Brother Richard, is it all right if I do this? Would it be okay if I did that?" That's the wrong question to ask. You should not be asking how close you can get to the world and still go to Heaven. You should be asking how close you can get to Jesus. That's the question you ought to be asking. You should not be asking how close you can get to Sodom and get away with it.

Don't you know that my wife, Jane, would slap my face if I was to come up to her and say, "Sweetheart, is it okay if I hold hands with another woman in church? We aren't going to go to bed or anything. You know I love you, Sweetheart; I just want to hold hands with somebody over there. Do you mind?" This is absurd to even think about. I wouldn't dare do that. I'm not that stupid. I want to keep my face on my head.

Yet we do the same thing to Jesus. "Jesus, I love You. Is it okay if I go hold hands with the world? Jesus, You know I'm not going to drink. You know I'm not going to smoke. Jesus, is it okay to go and see that movie? My friends are all after me to go with them. Jesus, I promise I'll close my eyes and my ears when the dirty parts come on." Give me a break, young person. What are you doing? That's hogwash. That's compromise. Compromise will get you in trouble. Lot started living a life of compromise and it cost him three things.

1. Lot lost his convictions.

The King James Version of Proverbs 1:10 says,

*My son, if sinners entice thee, **consent thou not.***

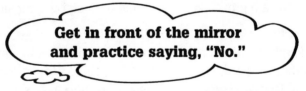

Get in front of the mirror and practice saying, "No."

I love the way the Scriptures say that: "Consent thou not." Some of you need to learn how to say "no" with some conviction. Some of you need to spend some time in front of a mirror practicing how to say "no," because some of you don't know how to say "no" very well. Some guy says, "Hey, sweetheart, let's go parking," and you say "no" as you start to unbutton your top blouse button. Give me a break. Get in front of the mirror and practice saying, "No. I consent not."

Let me tell you something else. Not everyone who is in church is a Christian. Beware. Some of the very people who will try to lure you into sin are the ones sitting next to you on the pew. Such people might be up front shouting and dancing when the praise and worship is going on. They might be in church every time the door is open.

> **If you ever try to get one of my teenagers to sin, I will get on you like ugly on the face of an ape!**

I tell my teenagers what to do if anybody in our church ever tempts them to go astray. If anybody ever encourages them to go out and get drunk; if anybody ever invites them to go smoke a cigarette or smoke dope; if anybody in our church ever asks someone to go with him or her to find a backseat somewhere, my young people are not only to say, "no," they are also to come straight to me. If anybody in our church is trying to tempt them to sin, my kids know that this boy right here will get on that person like ugly on the face of an ape.

Every one of us can slip and fall sometimes as we walk with Jesus. When any of my young people fall into sin, I want to be the first one to go and pick that teen up. But I will not put up with a person who is trying to lure somebody else away into sin.

Our problem is this: Most Christians have lived a life of compromise for so long that their consciences have become warped or seared. One of the most powerful portions of Scripture I think I have ever read is found in First Corinthians chapter 4, verses 3 through 5. Paul, an anointed man of God, is speaking here. Look at what he said:

I care very little if I am judged by you or by any human court; indeed, I do not even judge myself.

My conscience is clear, but that does not make me innocent. *It is the Lord who judges me.*

*Therefore judge nothing before the appointed time; wait till the Lord comes. He will bring to light what is hidden in darkness and will **expose the motives of men's hearts.** At that time each will receive his praise from God.*

"My conscience is clear, but that does not make me innocent." That's a heavy statement: "that does not make me innocent." "Wait a minute," you might be saying. "I thought you just live by your conscience." No. That's a lie. The Bible does not teach us to live by our conscience only, but by the Word of God. Walt Disney is the one who taught us to live by our conscience. Remember Pinocchio, bless his little wooden head. He was a puppet who became a boy. When the Fairy brought Pinocchio to life, she gave him Jiminy Cricket as his conscience. During this part of the movie you hear this catchy tune telling Pinocchio to "Give a little whistle...and always let your conscience be your guide." That sounds real good, doesn't it? But the problem is that our consciences are warped and seared.

You have grown up in a wicked world. You have grown up in a perverted society, and whether or not you realize it your conscience has been warped from the time you were born. Therefore, you cannot let your conscience be your guide.

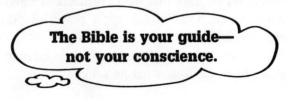

**The Bible is your guide—
not your conscience.**

The Bible is your guide—not your conscience. Young people come to me and say, "I don't feel guilty about it. I don't see anything wrong with having sex. Brother Richard, we're in love." To which I reply, "I don't care whether you feel guilty or not. What does the Bible say?"

No. You can't live by your conscience. Your conscience is warped. That's the reason it is so important that you are in the Book every day. You need to get in the Bible—it will straighten out that warped, seared conscience inside you.

Proverbs 12:15 teaches us that the way of a fool is right in his own eyes, but a wise person will listen to advice. Proverbs 21:2 says that a person's ways seem right to him, but God ponders—He weighs and tries—our hearts. It is amazing how we can all justify our own sin. We look at somebody else's sin and weaknesses and say, "They just need to get right with God." Then we look at our sin and say, "My sin is not as bad as his sin." We have a way of justifying our own failures and weaknesses. We are able to make it seem right in our own eyes, but God sees sin as sin.

> **If you live a life of compromise, one day you will find yourself doing things that you never thought you would do.**

Because of Lot's compromise, he lost his convictions and found himself doing things that he would have never dreamed of doing. You can't tell me that as his little girls were growing up, Lot would have said, "One day I'm going to offer those girls to a mob of sexual perverts to rape them and do whatever they want with them all night long." That is so unnatural for any father, even an ungodly father, to do. Yet back in Genesis 19:8 we find him doing that very thing. That's sick. No father in his right mind would do that. Lot was messed up. He was warped. His conscience was seared. Why? Because he set his tent near Sodom. And through that compromise, he lost every sense of conviction.

Some of you remember the first time you did an activity that you are still involved in; you remember how conviction swept over you. You said, "Dear God, I shouldn't be doing this." Conviction was beating away at your heart, but you pushed your way through it. The next time it was a little bit easier to ignore; the next even easier; and now you can go to a party straight from youth service. I've seen it. You can say, "Hand me that joint" with absolutely no conviction at all.

You get heavy with your boyfriend or girlfriend, petting in the backseat or in the bedroom. The first time you go, "Dear God, I shouldn't be doing this." Now you can do it and even go to the altar and shed false tears. Do you know what's happened? You've lost conviction. Your heart has grown cold and hard. Your conscience is warped. It is seared as if an iron seared it. You can't feel anything anymore.

2. Lot lost his testimony.

Lot found himself doing things he would have never thought he would do as a father. Not only did he lose his convictions, but, second, Lot lost his testimony. In verse 9 of Genesis 19, when Lot went out to talk to the people of the city, the people showed him absolutely no respect. They said, "Get out of our way or we will do to you worse than to them." The world hates hypocrites. They don't care if you go to church. They don't care if you are part of the choir. They don't care if you are in a discipleship program.

They could care less about all that stuff. If you are two-faced, they have absolutely no respect for you and you have lost your testimony.

Don't be a halfhearted Christian. Don't be a hypocrite. The only people whom Jesus actually got angry with were the hypocrites. He didn't get angry and blast the sinners; He blasted the hypocrites—the ones who said they were pure and yet were living an ungodly life.

In Revelation 3:15-16 the Lord said,

I know your deeds, that you are neither cold nor hot. I wish you were either one or the other!

So, because you are lukewarm—neither hot nor cold—I am about to spit you out of My mouth.

Some of your friends never take you seriously because you are so inconsistent. Are you one of those types of people? You get so on fire for Jesus that you make everybody nauseated. "I'm going to heal the sick. I'm going to do great things for God." You just talk Jesus, Jesus, Jesus. Then, three weeks later, you are smoking a joint or drinking or telling dirty jokes. Folks out there in the world are going, "He's messed up. He doesn't even know where he stands." Your inconsistency ruins your testimony.

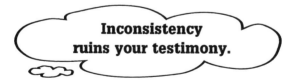

Inconsistency ruins your testimony.

Listen, all of us have ups and downs. Life can be a roller-coaster. All of us are going to have times when we are on the mountaintop, just so excited about Jesus, and other times when we are crying, "God, are You out there?" It is okay to be up and down sometimes; but here is what is not okay: being in and out. One day you are in with Jesus and the next you are out with the world. The next day you are in with Jesus and the next you are out with the world. I know that many of you want God to touch your school, but you don't stand for righteousness. Why don't you learn to have a backbone and be godly at school?

Some of you are just like Lot. You have lost your testimony because of your compromise. Remember what Lot's sons-in-law did when he told them that God was about to destroy the city? They laughed in his face. They said, "So when did God start talking to you, Lot? Was it in between those beers? Lot, that's so funny! God talked to you?!" The Scriptures say that they thought he was joking (see Gen. 19:14). They thought it was just another joke. Why? Because Lot's life gave no value to his testimony.

First Timothy chapter 4 is one of my favorite portions of Scripture. If you learn First Timothy 4:15-16, it will get you miles down the road of life. Paul was speaking to Timothy:

Be diligent in these matters; give yourself wholly to them, so that everyone may see your progress.

Watch your life and doctrine closely. Persevere in them, because if you do, you will save both yourself and your hearers.

Watch your life. Be consistent. Persevere through the hard times. Watch your doctrine—what you believe and what you teach. Watch the way you live, because then not only will you make it to Heaven, but everybody else who is watching you will make it to Heaven too. Many of us can't lead anybody to Jesus because we are constantly compromising.

3. Lot lost everything valuable to him.

Lot lost his convictions, Lot lost his testimony, and third, Lot lost everything valuable to him. If you will remember, I told you that Abraham and Lot split up in Genesis 13 because they were so blessed that the land couldn't support them both. God had blessed Lot so much in chapter 13. Yet in chapter 19 we see him fleeing for his life and having to leave all his possessions behind. Lot lost everything. Why? Because of his compromise.

When he was with Uncle Abraham, when he had Uncle Abraham constantly encouraging him to go to church and pushing him along, Lot served the Lord and God blessed him. But when he got out from beneath Abraham's protection and went on his own way, Lot started compromising, and he ended up losing everything that God blessed him with. Not only did he lose his possessions, but Lot even lost his wife.

In verse 26 of Genesis 19, Lot's wife did the very thing the angel had told them not to do: She looked back. The Scriptures say that no man who is going after Jesus should set his hands on the plow and then look back (see Lk. 9:62). If you are going to serve Jesus, then you are going to have to get your eyes off the pleasures of this world. My Bible tells me to fix my eyes on Jesus, the author and finisher of my faith (see Heb. 12:2). I want my eyes to be focused on Jesus.

The Bible says that the angels literally had to grab hold of Lot's hands and lead him out. The reason they did that was because Abraham prayed for Lot. Lot was saved because of Abraham. The Scriptures say that God remembered Abraham and so saved and delivered Lot (see Gen. 19:29). The angels literally had to grab Lot's hand, his wife's hand, and his two daughters' hands and drag them out of that city. Because Lot was a man of compromise, he even argued with the angels. He said, "Do I have to go all the way to the mountain? Let me just go to that little city over there."

Because Lot was a man of compromise, his wife was also filled with hesitation and compromise. She did not want to leave the pleasures of that world; so when she stopped to look back, she lost her life. She died and became a pillar of salt. And not only did Lot lose his possessions and his wife as a result of his compromise, it appears that he also lost his daughters. Genesis 19:30-38 tells how the daughters became so wicked that they got their father drunk and went to bed with him so they could have some kids. That's what it says! They got their daddy drunk and went to bed with him so that they could have kids. What a tragic result of compromise.

John 10:10 says that the thief comes to steal, kill, and destroy. The devil is out to kill you. If he can get you to compromise, he's got you right in the palm of his hand. Young people, let me tell you something. The devil is all the time throwing out a temptation for you. Listen to me! I'm trying to save you years of pain. If you give the devil an inch, he'll take a mile. If you start compromising with him, before long you will be doing things you never would have wanted to do. No child ever says, "When I grow up, I'm going to be a drunkard. When I grow up, I want to spend half of my life puking in gutters. When I grow up, I'm going to be a dope addict." Nobody thinks that is what will happen to him. How does it happen? It happens with one compromise. That first drink. You think that just one drink won't

hurt anything, but it leads to another and another and another. The next thing you know, your life is in shambles.

God is raising up a generation that is going to literally whip the devil's hiney. I believe that. God is raising up a generation that is becoming very serious. You are part of a generation that is sick and tired of religion. Church bores the living daylights out of you. You want the power of God in your life; you want the anointing of the Holy Spirit on you; you want to do great things for God. It only happens for those who will live a life of no compromise.

If you ever think that you are strong enough to be able to hang out near sin and get away with it, take a look at Judges chapters 13 to 16. Samson thought that he could compromise; he thought that he was strong enough that he could play with sin and not get caught. He played with Delilah and she would tie him up. The Bible tells us how, each time, Samson would shake things off and escape. But then came one of the saddest verses in the Bible, Judges 16:20:

> ...*He* [Samson] *awoke from his sleep and thought, "I'll go out as before and shake myself free." But he did not know that the Lord had left him.*

God wants to raise you up to do great and mighty exploits for Him, but it will not happen until you stop compromising. Some of you have things in your life that you need to deal with. Some of you are watching things that Jesus would never watch. Late at night when the family is in bed, you get up and go out to the living room or you turn on the TV in your bedroom and you watch things that should never be watched by a Christian. The next time you watch it, try asking Jesus to sit next to you and watch it with you. He'll never dent the cushion. Some of you need to get rid of the TV in your bedroom because you can't handle it. Some of you need to get rid of cable. How do I know? Because God has dealt with me about the same thing.

One of the most humiliating things that I have ever had to do is tell my children, Ashley and Caleb, that we had to disconnect cable because Daddy couldn't handle it. My kids are going, "But Daddy, we like *Little House on the Prairie* and all that kind of stuff." And I had to say, "Children, I'm so sorry, but I want to be a man of God and I just can't handle cable. I can't have that temptation so near to me." Some of you are going, "Wow, and I thought you were supposed to be a man of God." Well, I'm sorry, but I put on my britches one leg at a time, the same as every other guy. I'm a man of flesh and I have weaknesses too. I love what one of my young people said one time. He said, "Your greatest strength is to know your weakness."

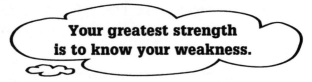

Your greatest strength is to know your weakness.

That made an impact on my life. *Your greatest strength is to know your weakness*—and to learn from it. If getting rid of basic cable wasn't hard enough, a couple of months later I had to tell my children that we had to disconnect the Internet. We had Internet access because Ashley and Caleb are home-schooled. I disconnected the Internet. Why? Because I couldn't handle it. There is just too much trash on the Internet. Now, I'm not saying that you are going to hell if you are connected to the Internet. You've got to judge your own life.

I told my children, "We've got to disconnect the Internet." They said, "Internet too? Why, Daddy?" Listen, it was the most humiliating thing I've ever had to do. "I'm sorry, kids, but we have to disconnect it because I want to be a man of God. I don't want to compromise; I want to live a holy life."

What I'm saying is that you've got a choice. You can play your games or you can get serious with God and live a life without compromise. Some of you have music, friends, videos, posters, ect., that are not pleasing to the Lord...you know what they are. I don't have to spell it out. The Holy Spirit is speaking to you and your mind is racing right now about things that only you know about. You've got to either deal with it or get left behind. I don't know about you, but I don't want to be a halfhearted Christian. I don't want to barely scrape through the pearly gates. I want to come in a blazing chariot.

> **Jesus is looking for a generation that wants to see how close they can live to Him while they are on earth.**

Jesus is looking for a committed generation. He is looking for a generation that is not trying to see how close they can live to the world and still get to Heaven. He is looking for a generation that wants to see how close they can live to Him while they are on earth.

My young friend, I have shared with you what God laid upon my heart. Now, it is time for you to respond.

I want you to pray a prayer with me, and I want you to understand that if you just pray this from your lips and don't mean it from your heart, then you are just wasting your breath. But if you mean it with your heart and follow it up with actions, then God will set you free. Some of you are bound by habitual sin that torments you so badly that you are sick and tired of compromise. It's time to say, "I just don't care anymore what people think. I'm going to live for Jesus." I invite you to get down on your knees right now, wherever you are, and pray this:

> **Dear Jesus, thank You for speaking to my heart. Thank You for not leaving me alone. Right now, I make a decision to no longer compromise. I will live for You and for You alone. Forgive me for my sin. Forgive me for compromising. Forgive me for hurting You, hurting others, and hurting myself. I ask that You wash me and cleanse me; remove from me all the guilt, all the stain, and all the condemnation. Come into my life as my Savior, my Lord, and my Best Friend. Jesus, from this day forward You can count on me. I will live for You every day of my life. In Jesus' name, amen.**

Praying that prayer was the easy part. The hard part is what you are going to do after you get up off your knees. Christianity is not just saying a prayer; Christianity is a decision to live like Jesus would live—every moment of every day. The Bible doesn't say, "Be sorry"; the Bible says, "Repent." Sorry is when you get caught with your hand in the cookie jar, but you have no intentions of changing. Repentance is when you are going in a certain direction; you recognize it is wrong; you stop; you turn 180 degrees; and you go the other direction. That's repentance. That's what Jesus is looking for. He is looking for a change in your life.

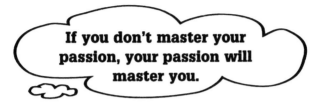

If you don't master your passion, your passion will master you.

Get serious about serving God. Get serious about turning from your sin. You need to find someone to hold you accountable. Find a pastor or a strong Christian friend who will help you keep the commitment that you have made to the Lord. If you don't master your passion, your passion will master you. It will kill you. Lot lost everything. Why? Because he set his tent near Sodom. Live holy, young person.

Live a life of no compromise.

C h a p t e r 8

What's All the Shouting About?

Recently at a baptism service here at Brownsville, a man went absolutely nuts right in the middle of the aisle. He was screaming at the top of his lungs and dancing up and down. People were looking over at him like, "Will somebody please settle that guy down?" What they didn't realize was that the lady in the baptismal tank was his wife. She had been out running around on him. He, meanwhile, had been faithful to her and was believing that God would bring her home. Now here she was dedicating her life to God. My lands, he had a *right* to rejoice! He had a *right* to be excited!

People ask, "Why do you have to be so noisy over there at that church? What's all the shouting about?" My friend, as we look through the Scriptures, we find that God's people have been asked that question before. Look at First Samuel 4:5-8 (KJV):

*And when the ark of the covenant of the Lord came into the camp, all Israel shouted with a great **shout**, so that the earth rang again.* [The New International Version says, "the ground shook."]

*And when the Philistines heard the noise of the shout, they said, What meaneth the noise of this great **shout** in the camp of the Hebrews?* [In other words, "What's all the shouting about?"] *And they understood that the ark of the Lord was come into the camp.*

And the Philistines were afraid, for they said, God is come into the camp. And they said, Woe unto us! for there hath not been such a thing heretofore.

Woe unto us! who shall deliver us out of the hand of these mighty Gods? these are the Gods that smote the Egyptians with all the plagues in the wilderness.

The Philistines asked, "Hey! What's all the shouting about?" I think it's about time the world heard the sound of God's people shouting to Him!

Think back for a moment to "The Final Frontier" messages. Remember how I told you that we need to use our tongues to do what they were created to do, which is to worship God? Listen, if your tongue is busy praising the Lord, then it won't have time to get you into trouble. One of the most powerful ways you can use your tongue, and so gain control of your "final frontier," is to *shout* unto God.

Look at Psalm 47:1-5 (KJV):

O clap your hands, all ye people; **shout** *unto God with the* **voice of triumph.**

For the Lord most high is terrible; He is a great King over all the earth.

He shall subdue the people under us, and the nations under our feet.

He shall choose our inheritance for us, the excellency of Jacob whom He loved. Selah. [Think about it.]

God is gone up with a **shout,** *the Lord with the sound of a trumpet.*

> **God has created each of us with built-in pressure valves to release built-up emotions.**

God has created each of us with built-in pressure valves to release the built-up emotions inside us. One pressure valve is crying. Whenever you just break down and cry, there is a release of emotion. I love to cry. Don't you? If I don't have a good cry every once in a while, I say, "God! I want you to break me; help me just cry, God! I need a good cry!"

Another pressure release is laughter. Medical professionals have proven that laughter releases healing endorphins into our bodies. They have simply discovered what the Bible has said all along—that laughter is good medicine (see Prov. 17:22). I love to laugh. I love being around funny people; I love a good joke; I love it when God touches me and sets me to laughing.

The third pressure valve is shouting. When God created us, He knew that we would have to release the emotions that build up inside us. Have you ever wanted to get off alone somewhere and just shout and scream? Every once in a while I get so frustrated, and pressure builds up inside me so much, that I know I'd better get off alone and do some shouting before I accidentally blast off at my wife or my kids or my staff, just from the intensity of the pressure. Listen, if you ever see me walking down the road with a red face and open mouth, just leave me alone; I'm shouting. You might think that I'm weird, but hey, just leave me alone! I'm happy!

AGHHH! AGHHHH! AGHHHHH!

There have been times when I have gone into a room, turned off the lights, and just yelled,

AGHHH! AGHHH! AGHHHHH! AGHHHHHH! AGH! AGH! AGHHH! AGH! AGH! AGHHHHHH!

And then I come out and say, "Whew! Now I feel better. Now I feel good! Now I can go out and love people again!" And every once in a while when people act like jerks, I just go back into my little room and scream some more. If you've never done this, try it. But don't do it when there's a psychiatrist around; they'll lock you up, my friend. Get off alone somewhere and use the pressure release valve of shouting. It works.

Prayer is a powerful way for you to experience all three release valves. When you pray, there are times when you cry, times when you laugh, and times when you shout. Prayer is the perfect way to release the pressures of life.

Have you ever noticed how people love to shout? Have you ever wondered why? For example, why do people love to shout at sports events? I observed one of Brownsville's youth ushers watching the last Super Bowl game on TV. I saw him standing on his chair, screaming at the top of his lungs (as if the team could even hear him). He was screaming and going bananas. Why do people like to do that?

Why do people like to go to rock concerts and scream and carry on like idiots? Listen, if we were to take a person out of the stadium or out of the rock concert and put him out on the street and let him act that same way, I guarantee that someone will come along real fast and lock the guy up.

Why do people come to revival meetings and shout? Why do they yell, "Go, Jesus! Go, Jesus!"? It is because shouting fulfills a spiritual need within us to worship.

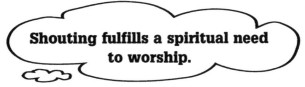

Shouting fulfills a spiritual need to worship.

Everyone worships something. God created us as spiritual beings; we were created with a *need* to worship something bigger than ourselves. Some folks say, "I don't believe in God. I don't worship anybody or anything." That is a lie; they *do* worship! Watch them at a football game, worshiping a pigskin. Watch them worship the singer at the rock concert. People feel the need to release the shout of worship that is built inside them. They actually need to feel the "high" of this release when worshiping God, but instead, too many people just experience it at football games or basketball games or rock concerts. They go from one spiritual experience to another, substituting artificial things for the real thing. There is a need in every person to express the shout of worship.

There is something very exhilarating about being in a packed stadium or auditorium with a crowd of shouting, excited people. Have you ever heard a sports announcer say, "We've got to take the crowd out of the game." Why do they say that? Do they want to get the fans out of the stadium? No, that is how they get their money. Are they wanting to get the crowd off the field? No, they are saying that there is an energy, an excitement, a power that is released when a crowd is cheering you on.

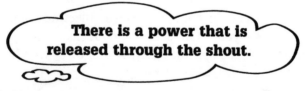

There is a power that is released through the shout.

Some of you experience this when you go witnessing. You might be out with four or five of your buddies and they turn to you and say, "I bet you would never go and witness to that guy over there!" Listen, by yourself you would never talk to that person, but now you have a crowd egging you on. You have a crowd going, "Come on, man, go! Go witness to that guy! Go tell him about Jesus!" And you start rolling up your sleeves and gritting your teeth and saying, "Let me at 'im!" Power is released when people lift up their voices together. Power is released through the shout.

I have noticed different kinds of shouts in the Bible. One portion of Scripture, in particular, Exodus 32:17-18, mentions four kinds of shouts.

*When Joshua heard the noise of the people shouting, he said to Moses, "There is the sound of **war** in the camp."*

*Moses replied: "It is not the sound of **victory**, it is not the sound of **defeat;** it is the sound of **singing** [rejoicing] that I hear."*

There are also different reasons for shouting. I have identified five reasons people shout. The first two are negative, and I pray that you never participate in these kinds of shouts.

The Delusive Shout (False Cry)

This is an empty shout. This is when we shout for no reason; our shout has no substance to it. At the beginning of this chapter we looked at First Samuel 4, where the ark of the covenant was returning to Israel. The people were shouting because they thought that the presence of God was back with them. But it was actually a delusive shout, a false cry. If you turn back in your Bible to First Samuel 3, you will see Israel's sinful condition. Eli the priest was backslidden, his sons were living in gross sin (verse 13 in chapter 3 says they "made themselves contemptible"), and there was darkness and despair throughout the land.

In First Samuel chapter 4, verse 3, the leaders of Israel said, "Let's go and get the ark. Let's go get God back." When the Philistines heard about this, they were scared at first, but then, in verse 9, they rallied themselves and went out to fight the Israelites. Look at verses 10 and 11. It is a sad story.

So the Philistines fought, and the Israelites were defeated and every man fled to his tent. The slaughter was very great; Israel lost thirty thousand foot soldiers.

The ark of God was captured, and Eli's two sons, Hophni and Phinehas, died.

Israel was backslidden. They thought that all they had to do was go and get the ark, and God would be with them. Everything would be all right. They didn't want to repent and turn away from their sins; they just wanted God to come bail them out of their problems.

It is possible to shout as a result of peer pressure, but that shout is empty and meaningless. I have watched my young people bring their friends to revival meetings. I've watched them drag those teenagers right up to the front row, right in front of Evangelist Steve Hill; and I've watched the discomfort and even panic in their eyes as they looked around. Then the music starts, Lindell Cooley steps up to the mike, and we have *church*! We start clapping and jumping and shouting, and those teenagers don't have much of a choice—they start clapping too. Gradually they get caught up in what's going on and join right in shouting, but it is an empty, delusive shout. It is a false cry.

Sinners can shout in revival, but it doesn't mean that God is working in their lives. Listen, just because the ark, or *revival,* has been brought to our city, that does not mean we can shout the shout of victory. There are no shortcuts. My friend, we must deal with the sin issues in our lives before we can shout about anything.

The children of Israel did not want to repent; they wanted to take a shortcut. They went and got the ark and shouted so loud that the ground shook. They just knew that they were going to be victorious; they just knew that they were gonna go stomp some hiney. But it was a delusive, empty shout and it had no effect.

The Destructive Shout (Evil Cry)

Acts 7:54-58 tells the story of the evil, destructive shout against Stephen:

When they heard this, they were furious and gnashed their teeth at him.

But Stephen, full of the Holy Spirit, looked up to heaven and saw the glory of God, and Jesus standing at the right hand of God.

"Look," he said, "I see heaven open and the Son of Man standing at the right hand of God."

*At this they covered their ears and, **yelling at the top of their voices,** they all rushed at him,*

dragged him out of the city and began to stone him. Meanwhile, the witnesses laid their clothes at the feet of a young man named Saul.

Think about what Jesus experienced. Look at Mark 15:13:

*"Crucify Him!" they **shouted.***

"Why? What crime has He committed?" asked Pilate.
But they shouted all the louder, "Crucify Him!"

These are two examples of evil, destructive, and angry cries. Members of Brownsville's youth group have experienced this. They have had people at school come up to them and get in their face and yell, "Don't tell me about Jesus again! I don't want to hear about it. Just go to blankety-blank-blank-blank!" People scream slanders and evil curses at them.

> **The people who screamed for your head yesterday may be screaming for your help today.**

Young person, never forget this: The people who screamed for your head yesterday may be screaming for your help—screaming for your heart—today. The very people who will burn a Bible and throw it in your face—the very ones who cursed you yesterday—may turn around and cry out for your help today. Listen to me. You don't know what might have happened in their lives in the last 24 hours. You don't know if maybe their parents split up last night. You don't know if that young man's daddy came home drunk last night and beat the living daylights out of him. You don't know if that young lady went to the abortion clinic after school yesterday and had an abortion, and now today she is hurting desperately.

You be careful, young person. Don't write people off just because of how they treated you yesterday. When you see them coming down the hall today, don't walk on by because you think they're going to curse you out again. You don't know what they're thinking. You don't know if they are hoping that you will stop them and talk to them about Jesus just one more time. You don't know how badly they are hurting inside. Don't ever forget that. If you are not careful, you might walk right by people when they need you the most.

I got radically saved in high school and my friends dropped me like a hotcake. They made fun of me and called me things like "preacher man" and "goody-two-shoes"; but listen, when they were hurting, they would pull me aside and ask for my help. I remember that the teacher who taught me how to smoke dope was the same teacher who snatched me out of class one day and said, "Richard, I wish I could serve Jesus like you do."

We read about the stoning of Stephen in Acts 7. Just a little bit later, in Acts 9, Saul was screaming out to God for help. The thief on the cross beside Jesus first screamed curses at Him (see Mt. 27:44), then later called out for His mercy (see Lk. 23:42).

The Desperate Shout (Frantic Heart Cry)

To You I call, O Lord my Rock; do not turn a deaf ear to me. For if You remain silent, I will be like those who have gone down to the pit.

Hear my cry for mercy as I call to you for help, as I lift up my hands toward Your Most Holy Place.
                                          Psalm 28:1-2

Two blind men were sitting by the roadside, and when they heard that Jesus was going by, they shouted, "Lord, Son of David, have mercy on us!"

*The crowd rebuked them and told them to be quiet, but they **shouted all the louder**, "Lord, Son of David, have mercy on us!"*

Jesus stopped and called them. "What do you want Me to do for you?" He asked.

"Lord," they answered, "we want our sight."

Jesus had compassion on them and touched their eyes. Immediately they received their sight and followed Him.

Matthew 20:30-34

The devil will tell you, "Don't even bother crying out to God. He's not going to listen to you. You've failed too many times." Those are lies from the pit of hell. Jesus always hears the desperate, frantic cry of one of His children. The Scriptures say that a broken, sincere heart will never be despised by the Lord (see Ps. 51:17). You just go ahead and cry, "Jesus! Help me!"

It kind of reminds me of the Tom and Jerry cartoons. Some episodes have this dog saying, "Listen, Jerry, if you ever need me to help you with that ole cat, just give a whistle. Just holler, and I'll be right by your side." Let's imagine that Tom is the devil, you are Jerry, and Jesus (forgive me, Lord) is the dog. I've seen some shows where Tom would do all kinds of things to try and stop Jerry from calling for help. He'd give him some bubble gum and then pounce on him.

That's what the devil will do—he will try to keep you from shouting. He wants to put a gag over your mouth to shut you up. Why? Because there is power released when we shout. The Lord hears the cry of His people. Steve Hill, the evangelist who speaks at every revival meeting here at Brownsville, says this:

> "A man's desperation for the presence of God should melt all preoccupation with self, notoriety, public image, and social status. His hunger and thirst, if genuine, will drive him to eat and drink regardless of the opinions of others. He will be willing to be a fool in the sight of his peers in order to be embraced in the arms of the Lord."

The Delightful Shout (Victory Cry)

*So all Israel brought up the ark of the covenant of the Lord with **shouts**, with the sounding of rams' horns and trumpets, and of cymbals, and the playing of lyres and harps.*

As the ark of the covenant of the Lord was entering the City of David, Michal daughter of Saul watched from a window. And when she saw King David dancing and celebrating, she despised him in her heart.
1 Chronicles 15:28-29

This time, when the ark of the covenant was brought, the people had repented. They had defeated their enemies, David was king, and they were ready for the glory of God to come home. There was such rejoicing going on that David forgot how he was "supposed to act" and started to dance and leap in the air. If you ever come to Brownsville and see me dancing like a maniac, and if you see my young people dancing with all their hearts and shouting to the Lord, you might just wonder why we're so fanatically excited. Listen, we have something to shout about! God has won the victory in our lives!

Look at Acts 3:8-10:

*He jumped to his feet and began to walk. Then he went with them into the temple courts, **walking and jumping, and praising God.***

When all the people saw him walking and praising God,

they recognized him as the same man who used to sit begging at the temple gate called Beautiful, and they were filled with wonder and amazement at what had happened to him.

> **The only way you can participate in the victory cry is to participate in the war.**

There is a victory shout in those whom the Lord has touched and set free. But let me tell you something. The only way you can participate in the victory cry is to participate in the war. Too many people sit on the sidelines. Again, let me use a sports event to help illustrate this point. You can jump up and down and shout, "We won! We won!" but *you* did not win, friend; your favorite team won. They were the ones working and practicing the past year. All you did was sit and watch. Listen, the reason some people don't get excited when souls are getting saved is because they are not participating in their salvation. If you want to experience the delightful shout, the victory cry, then start witnessing to people about Jesus. Then, when you see them coming down the aisle to receive the Lord, you can go ahead and get real excited! People around you just might wonder what's going on; they might even be downright critical, like Michal was about David back in First Chronicles.

Remember the guy I told you about at the beginning of this message, who was shouting when his wife got baptized? Listen to me, young person. Others will never understand your shouts of joy because they haven't faced your battles in life. People will never really know the depths of your gratitude to Him. Don't worry about it. Personally, I don't give a rip about what other people think of me. If I want to dance and have a good time because of what God has been doing in my heart and my life, I say, "Just leave me alone, Jack; I'm not dancing or shouting for you anyway! I'm shouting and dancing for Jesus."

> **Others will never understand your shouts of joy because they haven't faced your battles in life.**

The Determined Shout (Battle Cry)

*Judah turned and saw that they were being attacked at both front and rear. Then they **cried out** to the Lord. The priests blew their trumpets*

*and the men of Judah raised the **battle cry.** At the sound of their **battle cry,** God routed Jeroboam and all Israel before Abijah and Judah.*

2 Chronicles 13:14-15

*When the trumpets sounded, the people **shouted,** and at the sound of the trumpet, when the people gave a* *loud shout,* the wall collapsed; so every man charged straight in, and they took the city.

Joshua 6:20

I have a dear friend, Pastor Cary Robertson, who fought in several wars. I went to him and said, "Pastor Robertson, I'm about to teach young people about the different shouts in the Bible, and I have a question for you about the war cry. Do they, or do they not, teach soldiers to scream and shout when they are rushing at the enemy?"

"No, they don't teach soldiers to do that," he said. "We just did it naturally, and what it did was intimidate the enemy." He went on to say, "One of the most fearful sounds that I have ever heard in my life was when I was in a foxhole. I heard the opposing army strike up the trumpets and the drums, and I heard their voices echoing through the woods. A chill ran up and down my back. It was so scary as that army drew nearer; but listen, our natural response was to just jump right out of that foxhole and scream, **'aaghhhhhhh'** as we ran toward them. It was a determined war cry, and it was intimidating to the enemy."

> **One of the main purposes for the way cry is to intimidate the enemy.**

Many of you have been listening to the voice and rumblings of the enemy. The devil threatens, screams at, and curses you. Remember the story of David and Goliath? (Read First Samuel 17 if you don't.) Goliath spewed junk out from his mouth at David. "I'll kill you, boy. What are they doing sending a little dog out here to me?" The Bible says Goliath cursed David, but David shouted back, "I don't care what you say, Goliath! You may come at me with curses and slanders, but I come against you in the name of the Lord!"

Young person, listen to me! It's time you stopped listening to the devil yell his accusations and curses at you! It's time you let out a war cry! It's time you shouted a shout of victory! That shout will cause confusion in the enemy's camp. Look at what happened in Judges 7:20-22a:

*The three companies blew the trumpets and smashed the jars. Grasping the torches in their left hands and holding in their right hands the trumpets they were to blow, they **shouted,** "A sword for the Lord and for Gideon!"*

While each man held his position around the camp, all the Midianites ran, crying out as they fled.

When the three hundred trumpets sounded, the Lord caused the men throughout the camp to turn on each other with their swords.

First Peter 5:8 (KJV) says:

Be sober, be vigilant; because your adversary the devil, as a roaring lion, walketh about, seeking whom he may devour.

Listen, the only reasons a lion roars is because it is either wounded or old. A young, healthy lion sneaks up on its prey without its knowing he's there. The devil has been wounded. Every one of his teeth was snatched out of his jaws at Calvary! The Scriptures say that his power has been destroyed (see Col. 2:15), and he knows it. The devil knows that the only weapon he has against you is fear. So he gets in your face and roars. He tries to scare you.

When I was a little boy I walked to school every day. Along the way there was this little Chihuahua that used to run out and bark and snarl at my ankles like it was the fiercest dog in the world. That stupid little rat dog was so irritating, and one day I got sick and tired of it. When it came running out after me, I turned, and in a loud voice I said, **"RUFF! Ruff, ruff, RUFF, RUFF!"** Well, that little dog wheeled around with its tail between its legs and took off faster than the speed of light.

Young person, it's time to lift your voice. It's time to give a determined war cry and send the devil running. It's time to take authority over your own personal "final frontier" with a shout unto the Lord!

Final Words

Young person, I believe that you are part of the chosen generation that is going to roll out the welcome mat for the returning of the Lord Jesus Christ. I challenge you to move beyond fighting the battles of your flesh and move into the battlefield for the Lord. Allow Him to crucify the carnal desires that constantly haunt you, and begin to take your school and city for Jesus.

It is no mistake that society has labeled you Generation X. Yes, they call you Generation X because they want to blame you for their problems, and they do not see much value in many of your peers. However, God may be speaking prophetically over your generation.

As I mentioned in Chapter 5, I believe that there are four possible reasons why you are Generation X. First, you are going to experience Christ in a whole new and personal way. Because you are "Generation Christ," you are going to flow in a level of anointing that has not been experienced in the Christian world for years. You are going to receive an anointing that is going to break the yoke of oppression and the curse of sin over our nation and the nations around the world. You will prepare the Church to become the glorious Church that Christ is coming back for, a Church without spot or wrinkle.

Second, you are Generation X because you are the unknown factor that will find the solutions to our world's problems. Far from being the world's problem, as our society assumes that you are, you will solve the world's problems, turning nations back to truth and setting them free from the curse of sin and death.

Third, you are Generation X because you are a generation of great treasure waiting to be discovered. Much potential is buried beneath the outward facade presented by many of your peers. You will teach the Church by example to look beyond the physical appearance to the person within, recognizing that each is precious in Jesus' eyes.

Lastly, you are Generation X because you will harvest the world for Jesus. I believe that we are about to see history repeated as it is recorded in the Book of Acts. Churches everywhere are beginning to see people answer altar calls for repentance as the Lord adds to the Church daily those who are to be saved (see Acts 2:47). This, however, is but the beginning. Even as Acts 6:7 describes the Church as multiplying, so we are on the verge of a great awakening that is coming to all nations. Local churches that preach the true gospel and allow the Holy Spirit to move freely within their people are going to see multitudes coming into their congregations.

And do you know who is going to lead the way? You! Generation X! The teenagers who are ready to know their God and do great exploits!

Arise, young person! Allow Jesus to have full control of your heart, your ambitions, and your desires. Allow Him to raise you up as a vital part of His final army. Truly, you have come to the Kingdom of God for such a time as this! You have a purpose to fulfill in your generation! Arise and conquer. Let Jesus be Lord. It's time!

D Destiny Image
Revival Books

IT'S TIME
by Richard Crisco.
"We say that 'Generation X' does not know what they are searching for in life. But we are wrong. They know what they desire. We, as the Church, are the ones without a revelation of what they need." It is time to stop entertaining our youth with pizza parties and start training an army for God. Find out in this dynamic book how the Brownsville youth have exploded with revival power...affecting the surrounding schools and communities!
ISBN 1-56043-690-5 $9.99p

LET NO ONE DECEIVE YOU
by Dr. Michael L. Brown.
No one is knowingly deceived. Everyone assumes it's "the other guy" who is off track. So when people dispute the validity of current revivals, how do you know who is right? In this book Dr. Michael Brown takes a look at current revivals and at the arguments critics are using to question their validity. After examining Scripture, historical accounts of past revivals, and the fruits of the current movements, Dr. Brown comes to a logical conclusion: God's Spirit is moving. *Let No One Deceive You!*
ISBN 1-56043-693-X $10.99p

THE GOD MOCKERS
And Other Messages From the Brownsville Revival
by Stephen Hill.
Hear the truth of God as few men have dared to tell it! In his usual passionate and direct manner, Evangelist Stephen Hill directs people to an uncompromised Christian life of holiness. The messages in this book will burn through every hindrance that keeps you from going further in God!
ISBN 1-56043-691-3 $9.99p

A TOUCH OF GLORY
by Lindell Cooley.
This book was written for the countless "unknowns" who, like Lindell Cooley, are being plucked from obscurity for a divine work of destiny. Here Lindell, the worship leader of the Brownsville Revival, tells of his own journey from knowing God's hand was upon him to trusting Him. The key to personal revival is a life-changing encounter with the living God. There is no substitute for a touch of His glory.
ISBN 1-56043-689-1 $9.99p

Available at your local Christian bookstore.

Internet: http://www.reapernet.com

Destiny Image
Revival Books

WHEN THE HEAVENS ARE BRASS
by John Kilpatrick.
Pastor John Kilpatrick wanted something more. He began to pray, but it seemed like the heavens were brass. The lessons he learned over the years helped birth a mighty revival in Brownsville Assembly of God that is sweeping through this nation and the world. The dynamic truths in this book could birth life-changing revival in your own life and ministry!
ISBN 1-56043-190-3 $9.99p

WHITE CANE RELIGION
And Other Messages From the Brownsville Revival
by Stephen Hill.
In less than two years, Evangelist Stephen Hill has won nearly 100,000 to Christ while preaching repentance, forgiveness, and the power of the blood in what has been called "The Brownsville Revival" in Pensacola, Florida. Experience the anointing of the best of this evangelist's life-changing revival messages in this dynamic book!
ISBN 1-56043-186-5 $9.99p

PORTAL IN PENSACOLA
by Renee DeLoriea.
What is happening in Pensacola, Florida? Why are people from all over the world streaming to one church in this city? The answer is simple: *Revival!* For more than a year, Renee DeLoriea has lived in the midst of the revival at Brownsville Assembly of God. *Portal in Pensacola* is her firsthand account of this powerful move of the Spirit that is illuminating and transforming the lives of thousands!
ISBN 1-56043-189-X $9.99p

FROM HOLY LAUGHTER TO HOLY FIRE
by Dr. Michael L. Brown.
America is on the edge of a national awakening—God is responding to the cries of His people! This stirring book passionately calls us to remove the roadblocks to revival. If you're looking for the "real thing" in God, this book is must reading! (A revised edition of *High-Voltage Christianity*.)
ISBN 1-56043-181-4 $9.99p

Available at your local Christian bookstore.

Internet: http://www.reapernet.com

Prices subject to change without notice.   2:50

D *Destiny Image*
New Releases

CHILDREN OF REVIVAL
by Vann Lane.
What do you do with hundreds of children during services that last for hours? At first Pastor Vann Lane thought he would use all his usual "stuff" to entertain the children. The Lord thought differently. In this book you'll read remarkable stories of Brownsville Assembly's 11-year-old leader, the worship band of young musicians, and the 75-member prayer team of children between ages 8 and 12 years old. *Children of Revival* will forever change the way you view the Church's little members.
ISBN 1-56043-699-9 $9.99p

FOR GOD'S SAKE GROW UP!
by David Ravenhill.
It's time to grow up...so that we can fulfill God's purposes for us and for our generation! For too long we've been spiritual children clinging to our mother's leg, refusing to go to school on the first day. It's time to put away childish things and mature in the things of God—there is a world that needs to be won to Christ!
ISBN 1-56043-299-3 $9.99p

MORE THAN A CONQUEROR
by Howard Bell.
Despite being diagnosed with a fatal disease at the age of one, despite not being expected to live beyond age five, Howard Bell grew up to become *More Than a Conqueror*! This heartwarming story tells how the author, weighing only 45 pounds, triumphed in Christ to become an evangelist and the founder and president of his own ministry. An inspiring autobiography!
ISBN 1-56043-302-7 $9.99p

THE YOUNG WARRIORS
by Wesley Smith.
Today more than ever believers need to rise up and be people of courage in service to God! Learn what it takes to be a warrior in God's army and to slay the giants arrayed against the Church. God needs you in this end-time harvest to fulfill the Great Commission!
ISBN 1-56043-296-9 $9.99p

Available at your local Christian bookstore.

Internet: http://www.reapernet.com